THE YACHTSMAN'S GUIDE TO

# coastwise navigation

by Stafford Campbell

YACHTING/BOATING BOOKS · ZIFF-DAVIS PUBLISHING
COMPANY                                    NEW YORK

# Contents

# Introduction

*Navigation* can be defined as the process of directing the movement of a vessel from one point to another. Coastwise navigation, or "piloting," is that performed in inshore, or "pilot" waters, usually in the vicinity of the coastline of a body of water. In its long history—thought to date back some six to eight thousand years—the *art* of navigation has evolved almost into a *science* of navigation as we know it today. But "almost" is an important word since, in Bowditch's view, "The *science* of navigation can be taught, but the *art* of navigation must be acquired." Thus, knowledge, which I hope to impart to you in this book, reinforced by the experience you will gain in practicing the craft, will form the basis of your qualification as a practical navigator.

You are not going to find coastwise navigation to be an occult art. In fact, on almost every automobile trip you take, you are already practicing a number of the fundamentals. You depart from a known location, road map in hand, and follow a prescribed route to your planned destination. You observe the traffic rules along the way and, from time to time, confirm your progress by road signs, prominent landmarks or intersections until you arrive, safe and sound, at the appointed time.

While the sea is a much more variable environment than a paved highway, the navigation principles are similar. You depart from a known (charted) position, steer a given course, check your position with reference to navigational aids or landmarks, adjust your course as necessary to avoid dangers and arrive safely at your intended destination on schedule.

If my comments appear to imply planning and attention to detail in the course of a voyage, then the message is getting across. The Navy calls it "forehandedness," in describing the planning and care to anticipate events before they occur, so that solutions become part of your normal procedure rather than misadventures. Precise navigation can be one of the real pleasures and satisfactions of yachting, and to paraphrase John Curran, "Eternal vigilance is the price of safety at sea."

In the organization of this book, the first four chapters have been devoted to the tools of the trade; those you use for planning purposes, those you will need aboard and those outside the ship which are useful for your guidance and safety. Chapters 5 and 6 describe the techniques involved in conducting a coastwise voyage and are important to study carefully and to understand thoroughly. The remaining chapters discuss special situations or evolutions you will encounter and some of the tricks of the trade. You probably have a seaman's vocabulary already but, to clarify some of the specialized terms used in the text, a glossary is included at the end. In the Appendix are extracts from Chart No. 1, a compendium of the symbols and abbreviations approved for use on U.S. Charts and an illustration of the system of navigational aids in United States waters. You may wish to consult this reference material as you go along.

The objective of this book is to be as clear and concise as possible, concentrating on the information and techniques of immediate, practical interest to the yachtsman engaged in coastwise navigation. Should your study and experience whet your appetite for more—as well it might—the encyclopedic, classic texts on navigation—"Bowditch," *American Practical Navigator* (Defense Mapping Agency Hydrographic Center, Washington, 2 Vols.), and "Dutton," *Dutton's Navigation & Piloting* (Naval Institute Press, Annapolis, Maryland)—contain a lifetime of learning and are splendid reference volumes. Both volumes are discussed further in Chapter 1.

When your voyages take you offshore, you will find the sequel to this text in its companion volume, *The Yachtsman's Guide to Celestial Navigation* (Ziff-Davis Publishing Company, New York).

Welcome aboard!

# 1. Charts & Publications

The navigator's chart is his road map and no prudent seaman goes to sea without one. In early times, charts of the sea were published privately and jealously guarded. The information they provided, often obtained at the expense of fortunes and lives, could be of great strategic and commercial value. By the late eighteenth century, the governments of the leading maritime nations had begun to play an increasing role in the collection and dissemination of navigational data which, following the lead of the Royal Navy in 1823, was eventually to be made available to mariners everywhere.

Almost all charts published today issue from government sources and they are truly miracles in the information they convey. Charts of United States waters and possessions are published by the National Ocean Survey (NOS), a branch of the National Oceanic and Atmospheric Administration (NOAA) of the Department of Commerce in Washington. These are the charts you will use principally in coastwise navigation. A catalog folder of the charts and NOS publications covering the area in which you will be sailing, and which also lists the authorized sales agents in your locality, is available, without charge, from NOAA. A portion of a typical catalog is illustrated in Figure 1-1.

For Canadian coastal and Great Lakes waters, a similar area catalog is issued by the Canadian Hydrographic Service of the Department of Fisheries and the Environment, Ottawa, covering the nautical charts and related publications of that agency.

Should you be planning to voyage beyond coastal waters, you can obtain the *Catalog of Nautical Charts,* Pub. No. 1-N, for the region in which you are interested from the Defense Mapping Agency Hydrographic Center (DMAHC), Washington, the successor to the time-honored U.S. Navy Hydrographic Office.

Charts of Inland Rivers of the United States, not included in the NOAA lists, are available from the appropriate District Office of the U.S. Army Corps of Engineers.

Navigators are obviously encouraged to use up-to-date charts and, between acquisition of new editions, to use the *Weekly Notice to Mariners* published by the Defense Mapping Agency Hydrographic Center which provides information for updating charts and publications of the DMAHC, the National Ocean Survey and the U.S. Coast Guard. Each Coast Guard District also issues a *Local Notice to Mariners* advising of changes affecting the safety of navigation in that District. Small vessels using inshore waters not frequented by ocean-going commerce, or routes such as the Intracoastal Waterway, will find the local notices their principal, if not only, source of information.

*Figure 1–1. Specimen panel from NOAA Nautical Chart Catalog, Atlantic and Gulf Coasts, January, 1978.*

NAUTICAL CHART CATALOG 1
UNITED STATES
ATLANTIC AND
GULF COASTS
Including Puerto Rico and the Virgin Islands

ST. CROIX RIVER TO SANDY HOOK

# GENERAL INFORMATION

## PURCHASE AND ISSUE

## CHART PRICES

## CLASSIFICATION OF CHARTS
SMALL-CRAFT CHARTS

## CONVENTIONAL CHARTS

## NOTES, SYMBOLS, AND ABBREVIATIONS

## IMPORTANCE OF UP-TO-DATE CHARTS

## DATES ON CHARTS

## PUBLICATIONS RELATING TO NAUTICAL CHARTS
PUBLISHED AND ISSUED BY THE NATIONAL OCEAN SURVEY
UNITED STATES COAST PILOTS

## TIDE TABLES

## TIDAL CURRENT TABLES

## TIDAL CURRENT CHARTS

## TIDAL CURRENT DIAGRAMS

Modern nautical charts are goldmines of information and, if you are not already thoroughly familiar with them, your careful study before you venture forth is well merited. The selection of the best chart for your specific voyage may be a little confusing at first but, usually, you will want the one having the largest scale for the area you will be navigating. For coastwise navigation, the scale groups classified as *Coast Charts* and *Harbor Charts,* which have the largest scales and cover the smallest areas, will be used most often.

You may also find helpful the series of *Small-Craft Charts* which employ scales in their main panels and insets comparable to the coast and harbor charts they frequently duplicate. The principal features of the small-craft chart are the supplementary port facility information, specifically oriented to the small-boat operator, and the format which permits the chart to be folded into a number of convenient panels for easy handling in confined quarters. In some instances, such as for the Intracoastal Waterway, the format of the small-craft route chart is admirably suited to the navigator's need and, as a consequence, will eventually replace the corresponding conventional charts. As long as there is adequate space in which to work, I prefer the conventional, flat nautical chart, but in the open cockpit of a fast runabout the small-craft chart comes into its own.

In recent years, collections of charts, or "folios" as they are called, have been offered by private publishers covering some of the more popular cruising areas. The source of the data is almost always the government charts of the area and, sometimes, the original chart is actually reproduced, in whole or in part, adjusting the scale to fit the format. Additional information of interest to the cruising yachtsman may be superimposed on the chart reproductions—such things as recommended courses or facilities ashore—resulting in a handy and economical package. Since the government does not exercise control over the production of these private folios, reproduced charts are required to carry the legend, "NOT TO BE USED FOR NAVIGATION." With the cost of individual charts, and the time and effort required to keep a large inventory updated, an increasing number of yachtsmen are making use of the reproduced-chart folios for planning purposes when contemplating cruises into new waters.

A nautical chart presents, on a flat sheet of paper suitable for plotting, a graphic representation of the features of interest to the navigator, such as the depth of the water (called "soundings"), the location and character of the shoreline and off-lying dangers to navigation, prominent objects ashore which can serve as landmarks and aids to navigation. There is a myriad of supplementary data, such as the type of bottom, overhead clearances, improved channels, and so forth. Much of the information is presented in symbols and abbreviations so the navigator should develop the ability to recognize their meanings without hesitation. For a complete summary of the manner in which all the chart data are presented, make a thorough review of Chart No. 1, *Nautical Chart Symbols and Abbreviations,* an extract of which is included in the Appendix.

In Figure 1-2, a portion of a typical harbor chart, with an original scale of 1:20,000, is shown in reduced size to illustrate some of the more common symbols and abbreviations and the physical objects they represent. The utilization of this information will be discussed in more detail in Chapters 5 and 6, but it is worthwhile at this stage to become familiar with the system.

Since charted soundings are indicated by a single figure at each location, and since most coastal waters have some tide to contend with, it is necessary that the navigator recognizes the *chart sounding datum,* as it is

*Figure 1-2. Visualizing the symbols used on Nautical Charts.*

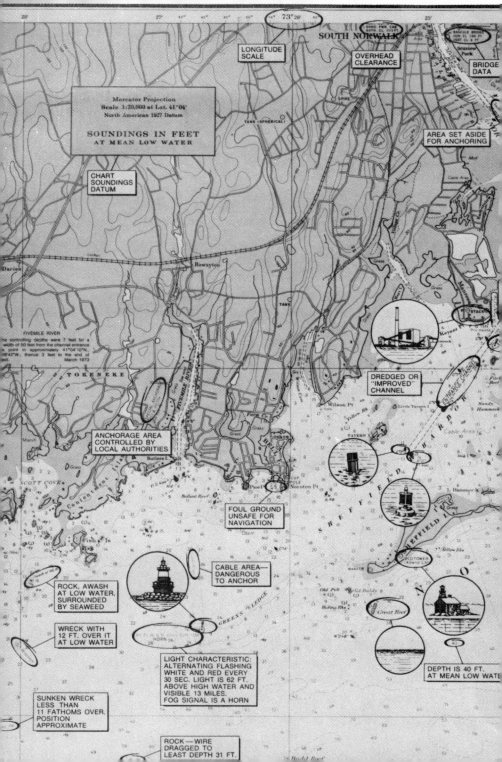

SOUTH NORWALK

LONGITUDE SCALE

OVERHEAD CLEARANCE

BRIDGE DATA

Mercator Projection
Scale 1:20,000 at Lat. 41°04'
North American 1927 Datum

SOUNDINGS IN FEET
AT MEAN LOW WATER

AREA SET ASIDE FOR ANCHORING

CHART SOUNDINGS DATUM

DREDGED OR "IMPROVED" CHANNEL

ANCHORAGE AREA CONTROLLED BY LOCAL AUTHORITIES

FOUL GROUND UNSAFE FOR NAVIGATION

CABLE AREA— DANGEROUS TO ANCHOR

ROCK, AWASH AT LOW WATER, SURROUNDED BY SEAWEED

WRECK WITH 12 FT. OVER IT AT LOW WATER

LIGHT CHARACTERISTIC: ALTERNATING FLASHING WHITE AND RED EVERY 30 SEC. LIGHT IS 62 FT. ABOVE HIGH WATER AND VISIBLE 13 MILES. FOG SIGNAL IS A HORN

DEPTH IS 40 FT. AT MEAN LOW WATER

SUNKEN WRECK LESS THAN 11 FATHOMS OVER. POSITION APPROXIMATE

ROCK — WIRE DRAGGED TO LEAST DEPTH 31 FT.

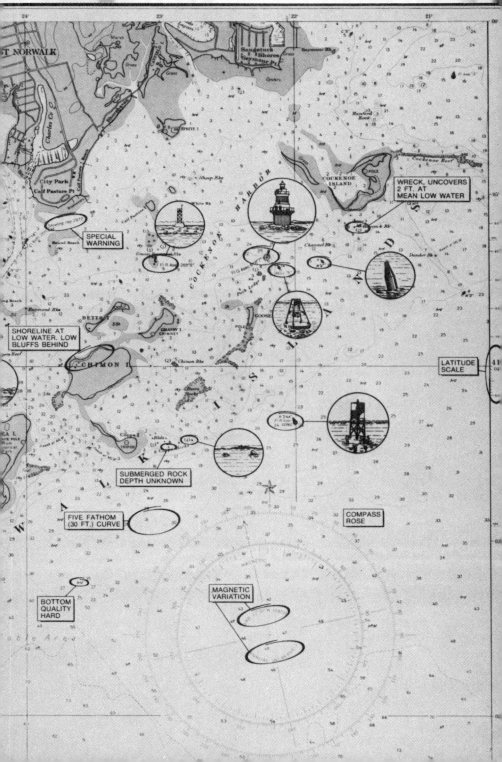

ST NORWALK

SPECIAL
WARNING

WRECK, UNCOVERS
2 FT. AT
MEAN LOW WATER

SHORELINE AT
LOW WATER. LOW
BLUFFS BEHIND

LATITUDE
SCALE

SUBMERGED ROCK
DEPTH UNKNOWN

FIVE FATHOM
(30 FT.) CURVE

COMPASS
ROSE

MAGNETIC
VARIATION

BOTTOM
QUALITY
HARD

called, which is used in the construction of the particular chart. In order to present the depths in the safest way, the datum is usually selected, and the soundings indicated, as of low water. For example, the NOS charts of the Atlantic and Gulf Coasts have adopted the chart datum of *mean low water* (MLW)—the average height of all low tides at the location. By use of the *Tide Tables,* discussed later in this chapter, the navigator can predict the depth at the time of passage. The chart sounding datum is stated in the legend on each chart such as, "Soundings in Feet at Mean Low Water." Always note, too, whether the charted depths are expressed in feet, meters or fathoms (six feet). Failure to do so has resulted in embarrassment.

You will notice at the right side and top of Figure 1-2, latitude and longitude scales by means of which any point on the chart can be located. Similar scales appear on both sides and at the top and bottom of conventional nautical charts. You may remember that latitude and longitude—derived from the Latin words for "breadth" and "length"—are the coordinates for identifying all locations on earth.

Latitudes, called "parallels" because they are all parallel to the equator, are, technically speaking, the angular distance from the equator, measured north or south from 0° to 90°. Longitudes, referred to as "meridians,"— probably stemming from the ancient Latin for "midday," when the sun crosses the longitude of the observer —are the angles formed at the poles between the prime meridian (0°) and that of the observer. Longitude is measured east or west from the prime meridian through 180°. Incidentally, 0°, the prime meridian, is located at the Greenwich Observatory in England where it was officially established by international agreement in 1884. It is now observed by all maritime nations and the longitudes on the charts you will use relate to the meridian of Greenwich.

Because navigators want to work on a flat sheet, while

we live on a globe, a way had to be found to represent the round earth on flat paper. Such a representation is called a "projection." Although there are a number of different projections possible—actually a study in itself —the one in common use by mariners, and for virtually all the charts you will use in coastwise navigation, is named the "Mercator projection" after a Flemish geographer who first published a chart embodying his principle in 1569.

Figure 1-3 illustrates schematically the theory of the Mercator chart, the projection having been developed by wrapping a flat sheet cylindrically around the earth at the equator and projecting the latitude and longitude lines upon it. In practice, the projection is expanded mathematically—a matter of technical interest, perhaps, but of little or no significance to the user.

The outstanding feature of the Mercator projection is that the latitude lines, normally parallel on earth, stay so, while the meridians of longitude, which actually converge as they approach the earth's poles, show on the chart equidistant from each other and perpendicular to the latitudes. This means that a vessel's course, plotted as a straight line, crosses every meridian at a constant angle, and that direction can be measured from any parallel or meridian—a great convenience. The only distortion in the true shape of a charted area is that the parallels of latitude appear slightly farther apart as the distance from the equator increases. For the purposes of coastal and harbor charts, however, this is hardly noticeable and is of no moment except in being sure to measure distance by the *adjacent* latitude scale. More about this later. The latitude and longitude on a Mercator chart also become convenient, "rectangular" coordinates, making it a simple matter to identify or plot any position by its N-S and E-W dimensions.

*Direction* in navigation is expressed as an angle measured clockwise from North (or the ship's head, if relative direction is wanted) through 360 degrees. In this

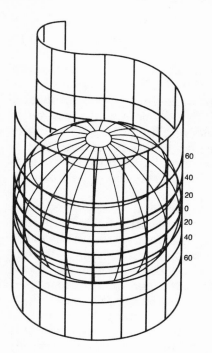

*Figure 1-3. The Mercator Projection—One way of showing the Round Earth on Flat Paper.*

scheme, East is designated as 90°—"090" in plotting parlance—Southwest as 225°, and so forth. In the old, sailing-ship days, a traditional way of stating direction was by "points," there being a total of 32 points, 11¼° apart. It was part of the sailor's art to be able to "box" the compass—naming all the points in order. Today, except for identifying directions in a general way, the point system has for practical purposes given way to the 360-degree mode.

In the chart reproduction in Figure 1-2, the compass rose indicates three direction systems simultaneously. The outer circle, divided into 360 degrees, measures *true* direction on the chart. The middle circle, also in degrees, indicates *magnetic* direction. (The difference between the two, known as "magnetic variation," will be discussed further in Chapter 3). The inner circle shows magnetic direction by the point system, the 32 points and 128 "quarter points" being indicated, though not named, by the graduations.

In coastwise navigation, courses and bearings are ordinarily plotted along a "rhumb line"—a line on the earth's surface which makes the same angle at every meridian. We have seen that such a line plots as a straight line on a Mercator chart, and a vessel proceeding on a rhumb line between two points maintains a constant compass heading.

*Distance* in coastwise navigation is measured, customarily, along the rhumb line connecting two points. For navigational purposes, one minute of latitude on the earth's surface is considered to average about 6,080 feet. It happens that the International Nautical Mile is about 6,076 feet, so, for convenience, practicing navigators have adopted the convention that *one minute of latitude equals one nautical mile.* This means that instead of having to refer to a mileage scale, you have a ready reference available in the latitude scales at either side of your chart. Remembering that on a Mercator chart the spacing of the parallels changes slightly with the distance from the equator, your mileage measurement should always be made on the latitude scale *adjacent* to the distance line you are measuring.

Although we have spoken first about charts, there are other publications which are valuable to consult when you go to sea. At the forefront of these are the *Tide Tables* which give the predicted times of high and low water and their heights, relative to the chart datum, for almost 200 reference ports around the world, and the tidal difference and other constants for about 6,000 more stations. The tables are published annually by the National Ocean Survey in four volumes covering the world.

Using the *Tide Tables* for approximating the level of the water, either to figure your margin of safety over a submerged obstruction, or under an overhead clearance, is an important, though simple, operation which you can follow in the tabular excerpts shown in Figure 1-4.

The upper part of Figure 1-4 is extracted from Table 1, Daily Tide Predictions, for the reference port of Portland, Maine. You can see, by inspection, that on Friday, November 17, 1978, high water occurs at 1224 (24 minutes after noon), and the height will be 9.6 feet above the chart datum which is mean low water. The following low tide occurs at 1848 (6:48 P.M. on the twelve-hour clock) and will be 0.6 feet *below* the datum. By comparing your time with the predicted times, you can approximate the state of the tide in between high and low water but, if greater accuracy is required, Table 3 in the back of the *Tide Tables* will provide it.

The lower part of Figure 1-4 is extracted from Table 2, Tidal Differences and Other Constants. Taking Friendship Harbor, No. 795, as an example, inspection will tell you that high water occurs eighteen, and low water eleven minutes earlier than at Portland. The heights of high and low water will be the same as Portland's, and the mean range between high and low tides is 9.0 feet. Extreme, "spring" tides at Friendship will range 10.4 feet. That's all there is to it, unless you happen to live in an area that is tide-free in which case you can dispense with the *Tide Tables* altogether.

A second publication, related to the *Tide Tables* and somewhat similar in design, is the *Tidal Current Tables,* popularly known, to avoid the inevitable confusion, as the "Current Tables." Excerpts from these tables, which are published annually in two regional volumes by the National Ocean Survey, are shown in Figure 1-5. The main tables show the daily predicted times of slack water and the velocities at maximum current, on both the flood and ebb, for a number of reference stations. A secondary table of differences allows similar predictions to be made for a large number of related stations in the general area.

To follow an example, at Hell Gate on Friday, November 17, 1978, you will find, in the upper part of Figure

TIMES AND HEIGHTS OF HIGH AND LOW WATERS

| | OCTOBER | | | | | | NOVEMBER | | | | | DECEMBER | | | |
|---|---|---|---|---|---|---|---|---|---|---|---|---|---|---|---|

| DAY | TIME h.m. | HT. ft. | DAY | TIME h.m. | HT. ft. | DAY | TIME h.m. | HT. ft. | DAY | TIME h.m. | HT. ft. | DAY | TIME h.m. | HT. ft. | DAY | TIME h.m. | HT. ft. |
|---|---|---|---|---|---|---|---|---|---|---|---|---|---|---|---|---|---|
| 1 SU | 0406 1014 1622 2232 | 0.1 9.1 0.0 9.2 | 16 M | 0430 1041 1659 2309 | -1.0 10.5 -1.4 9.9 | 1 W | 0440 1052 1711 2321 | -0.2 10.1 -1.0 9.3 | 16 TH | 0534 1143 1806 | 0.0 9.9 -0.8 | 1 F | 0457 1110 1736 2346 | -0.6 10.7 -1.7 9.5 | 16 SA | 0551 1200 1823 | 0.4 9.4 -0.5 |
| 2 M | 0440 1049 1659 2308 | -0.1 9.4 -0.3 9.3 | 17 TU | 0513 1126 1744 2355 | -0.8 10.4 -1.3 9.7 | 2 TH | 0521 1133 1756 | -0.3 10.3 -1.3 | 17 F | 0016 0611 1224 1848 | 8.8 0.3 9.6 -0.6 | 2 SA | 0545 1159 1825 | -0.7 10.8 -1.8 | 17 SU | 0034 0627 1237 1900 | 8.3 0.6 9.2 -0.3 |
| 3 TU | 0513 1122 1735 2345 | -0.2 9.6 -0.6 9.3 | 18 W | 0558 1208 1827 | -0.4 10.2 -1.0 | 3 F | 0006 0605 1217 1839 | 9.4 -0.4 10.4 -1.3 | 18 SA | 0057 0652 1303 1928 | 8.5 0.3 9.3 -0.3 | 3 SU | 0036 0636 1250 1915 | 9.5 -0.7 10.8 -1.7 | 18 M | 0110 0706 1315 1939 | 8.2 0.7 9.0 -0.1 |

TIME MERIDIAN 75° W.   0000 IS MIDNIGHT.   1200 IS NOON.
HEIGHTS ARE RECKONED FROM THE DATUM OF SOUNDINGS ON CHARTS OF THE LOCALITY WHICH IS MEAN LOW WATER.

TABLE 2.—TIDAL DIFFERENCES AND OTHER CONSTANTS                              207

| No. | PLACE | POSITION | | DIFFERENCES | | | | RANGES | | |
|---|---|---|---|---|---|---|---|---|---|---|
| | | Lat. | Long. | Time | | Height | | Mean | Spring | Mean Tide Level |
| | | | | High water | Low water | High water | Low water | | | |
| | | ° ′ N. | ° ′ W. | h. m. | h. m. | feet | feet | feet | feet | feet |
| | MAINE, Outer Coast Time meridian, 75°W. | | | on PORTLAND, p.32 | | | | | | |
| 779 | Tenants Harbor——————————— | 43 58 | 69 12 | -0 11 | -0 11 | +0.3 | 0.0 | 9.3 | 10.6 | 4.6 |
| 781 | Monhegan Island——————————— | 43 46 | 69 19 | -0 13 | -0 09 | -0.2 | 0.0 | 8.8 | 10.1 | 4.4 |
| 783 | Burnt Island, Georges Islands——— | 43 52 | 69 18 | -0 13 | -0 12 | -0.1 | 0.0 | 8.9 | 10.2 | 4.4 |
| | St. George River | | | | | | | | | |
| 785 | Port Clyde———————————————— | 43 56 | 69 16 | -0 11 | -0 07 | -0.1 | 0.0 | 8.9 | 10.2 | 4.4 |
| 787 | Otis Cove————————————————— | 43 59 | 69 14 | -0 15 | -0 14 | +0.1 | 0.0 | 9.1 | 10.5 | 4.5 |
| 789 | Thomaston————————————————— | 44 04 | 69 11 | -0 04 | -0 03 | +0.4 | 0.0 | 9.4 | 10.8 | 4.7 |
| 791 | New Harbor, Muscongus Bay——— | 43 52 | 69 29 | -0 10 | -0 05 | -0.2 | 0.0 | 8.8 | 10.1 | 4.4 |
| 793 | Muscongus Harbor, Muscongus Sound— | 43 58 | 69 27 | -0 09 | -0 03 | 0.0 | 0.0 | 9.0 | 10.4 | 4.5 |
| >795 | Friendship Harbor——————————— | 43 58 | 69 20 | -0 18 | -0 11 | 0.0 | 0.0 | 9.0 | 10.4 | 4.5 |
| | Nedomak River | | | | | | | | | |
| -- | Jones Neck | 44 07 | -- | | | | | | | |

*Figure 1–4. Using the Tide Tables—High Water occurs at Portland on November 17 at 1224 with a height of 9.6 feet and Low Water at 1848, 0.6 feet below the chart datum. High and Low Water for Friendship Harbor are shown as differences from the reference station.*

1-5, that slack water before the afternoon ebb begins, occurs at 1126. The maximum ebb current will take place at 1417 with a speed of 4.8 knots. The slack water occurs again at 1752, following which the current will

F-FLOOD, DIR. 050° TRUE    E-EBB, DIR. 230° TRUE

| | | NOVEMBER | | | | | | | DECEMBER | | | | | | |
|---|---|---|---|---|---|---|---|---|---|---|---|---|---|---|---|
| | SLACK WATER TIME | MAXIMUM CURRENT TIME VEL. | | | SLACK WATER TIME | MAXIMUM CURRENT TIME VEL. | | | SLACK WATER TIME | MAXIMUM CURRENT TIME VEL. | | | SLACK WATER TIME | MAXIMUM CURRENT TIME VEL. | |
| DAY | H.M. | H.M. | KNOTS | DAY | H.M. | H.M. | KNOTS | DAY | H.M. | H.M. | KNOTS | DAY | H.M. | H.M. | KNOTS |
| 1 W | 0339 0950 1607 2217 | 0018 0640 1239 1906 | 4.9E 3.9F 5.1E 3.9F | 16 TH | 0442 1044 1710 2309 | 0120 0744 1340 2007 | 4.8E 3.7F 4.9E 3.6F | 1 F | 0405 1012 1640 2240 | 0040 0705 1306 1933 | 5.1E 3.9F 5.3E 3.8F | 16 SA | 0501 1057 1729 2319 | 0131 0756 1350 2019 | 4.8E 3.5F 4.9E 3.4F |
| 2 TH | 0421 1034 1652 2302 | 0101 0722 1324 1949 | 5.0E 3.9F 5.2E 3.9F | 17 F | 0524 1126 1752 2351 | 0156 0823 1417 2047 | 4.7E 3.6F 4.8E 3.5F | 2 SA | 0454 1101 1730 2331 | 0129 0752 1357 2024 | 5.1E 3.9F 5.3E 3.8F | 17 SU | 0541 1137 1809 2359 | 0206 0833 1428 2057 | 4.7E 3.4F 4.8E 3.3F |
| 3 F | 0505 1120 1739 2350 | 0148 0809 1412 2037 | 5.0E 3.9F 5.1E 3.8F | 18 SA | 0607 1209 1835 | 0234 0903 1458 2129 | 4.6E 3.4F 4.7E 3.3F | 3 SU | 0547 1154 1824 | 0219 0845 1448 2115 | 5.1E 3.8F 5.2E 3.7F | 18 M | 0622 1217 1850 | 0245 0914 1507 2135 | 4.6E 3.3F 4.7E 3.2F |

TIME MERIDIAN 75° W.    0000 IS MIDNIGHT.    1200 IS NOON.

| | TABLE 2.—CURRENT DIFFERENCES AND OTHER CONSTANTS | | | | | | | | | | 145 |
|---|---|---|---|---|---|---|---|---|---|---|---|
| No. | PLACE | POSITION | | TIME DIFFERENCES | | VELOCITY RATIOS | | MAXIMUM CURRENTS | | | |
| | | | | | | | | Flood | | Ebb | |
| | | Lat. | Long. | Slack water | Maximum current | Maximum flood | Maximum ebb | Direction (true) | Average velocity | Direction (true) | Average velocity |
| | | ° ' N. | ° ' W. | h. m. | h. m. | | | deg. | knots | deg. | knots |
| | EAST RIVER | | | | | | | | | | |
| | Time meridian, 75°W. | | | on HELL GATE, p.40 | | | | | | | |
| 2060 | Between Willets Point and Throgs Neck- | 40 48 | 73 47 | -0 50 | -1 15 | 0.3 | 0.1 | 050 | 1.0 | 250 | 0.6 |
| 2065 | Cryders Point, 0.4 mile NNW. of------- | 40 48 | 73 48 | -0 30 | -0 50 | 0.4 | 0.2 | 110 | 1.3 | 285 | 1.1 |
| 2070 | Old Ferry Point------------------------ | 40 48 | 73 50 | -0 40 | -0 35 | 0.5 | 0.3 | 075 | 1.7 | 240 | 1.5 |
| 2075 | Clason Point, 0.2 mile SSW. of-------- | 40 48 | 73 51 | -0 10 | -0 40 | 0.5 | 0.3 | 070 | 1.8 | 250 | 1.5 |
| 2080 | Flushing Creek entrance--------------- | 40 46 | 73 51 | | Current weak and variable. | | | | | | |
| 2085 | Rikers I. chan., off La Guardia Field- | 40 47 | 73 53 | +0 05 | -0 05 | 0.3 | 0.3 | 090 | 1.1 | 260 | 1.3 |

*Figure 1–5. Using the Current Tables—Slack Water occurs at Hell Gate on November 17 at 1126, before the ebb begins, and at 1752, before the flood begins. The maximum currents occur at 1417 and 2047, at 4.8 and 3.5 knots respectively. The currents at Old Ferry Point are shown as differences from the reference station.*

flood, reaching its maximum velocity of 3.5 knots at 2047. The importance of having this information obviously comes in planning your passage through an area with as favorable a current as possible. The difference between the maximum ebb and flood at Hell Gate is 8.3 knots—a matter of critical interest to the navigator of a slow vessel.

The lower portion of Figure 1-5 shows some of the secondary stations whose predictions are related to Hell Gate. Taking, as an example, No. 2070, Old Ferry Point, you see that slack water occurs 40 minutes before Hell Gate, and maximum current 35 minutes before the reference station. The velocity at maximum flood, however, is only half that predicted for Hell Gate, while at maximum ebb, the velocity is only 0.3 of that of the reference station.

In Chapter 2, we will be discussing Aids to Navigation and Figure 2-1 shows excerpts from the Coast Guard *Light List*, a publication which describes in detail the navigational aids found in coastal waters. The *Light Lists* are issued annually, in five regional volumes, by the Department of Transportation, United States Coast Guard, and are sold by the Superintendent of Documents, U.S. Government Printing Office, Washington, and by many of the regular sales agents of the National Ocean Survey.

The principal information which the *Light List* provides, beyond that shown on the charts, is detailed data on lights and their time sequences, descriptions of the physical light structures for positive daytime identification, and the characteristics of fog signals. This publication includes additional information about the lesser navigational aids and has a comprehensive explanation section in its Introduction—the portions on radiobeacons being of special interest to yachtsmen.

Another NOAA publication with which you should be familiar, although you may not use it as often, is the *United States Coast Pilot*, the "Sailing Directions" for coastal waters. The *Coast Pilot* is designed to extend the navigational information presented on the charts and it is issued approximately annually in nine volumes covering all the coastal areas of the United States and its possessions. While of primary interest to operators of larger vessels, the *Coast Pilot* does contain, in handy form, useful information for the yachtsman such as Distress procedures (in the General Information section), Special Anchorage or Regulated Navigation Areas and their requirements, traffic lane usage, bridge opening signals and rules, canal regulations, Custom ports, harbors of refuge and general geographic data, all of which would be of particular value for a first cruise in strange waters.

The safe conduct of a voyage not only makes extensive use of the available navigational aids, but also the Rules of the Road—the "traffic laws" designed to prevent collisions between ships at sea. Although outside the scope of this volume, it is important that yachtsmen be familiar with the essentials. The latest International Rules, called the 72 COLREGS, came into force in 1977. They, as well as the Inland Rules, are summarized in the Coast Guard publication, *Navigation Rules,* CG-169, and ought to be part of every navigator's fund of knowledge.

Although not strictly part of his navigation procedure, weather is always of concern to the coastwise yachtsman. Nowadays, weather reports are usually as close as your radio receiver, but the schedules and frequencies often are not known. A useful publication in this respect is *Worldwide Marine Weather Broadcasts,* issued by NOAA's National Weather Service and the Naval Weather Service Command. The Canadian Coast Guard publishes a quarterly volume called *Radio Aids to Marine Navigation,* which also includes complete information on weather broadcasts in that country. It is available from Printing and Publishing, Supply and Services Canada, in Ottawa.

For the cruising yachtsman, there is a superabundance of commercially published cruising guides for most of the popular areas, specialized guides for interarea waterways like the Intracoastal and facilities lists to familiarize you with the services available at your destination. A number of these are excellent and you will find them a useful and pleasurable adjunct to your life afloat. The choice, however, is highly subjective and rapidly changing. As a consequence, many yachtsmen acquire only the most current editions and those best suited to their particular needs at the time of their departure, and don't attempt to maintain a complete and updated library.

On the subject of libraries, every student of navigation will want to have one or both of the classic reference texts mentioned in the Introduction. First and foremost is "Bowditch," *American Practical Navigator,* Pub. No. 9 of the Defense Mapping Agency Hydrographic Center, and available through their regular outlets. Called "an epitome of navigation," which it truly is, it was originally published by Nathaniel Bowditch (1773–1838) of Salem, Massachusetts, who was acclaimed as one of the outstanding mathematicians of his time. The copyright was acquired by the U.S. Navy Hydrographic Office in 1868 after some 66 years of successful publication, and the work continued through seventy editions in the century and a half of its existence. In 1972, the DMAHC assumed the responsibility for publishing the *American Practical Navigator* and it has recently been reissued in two volumes, basically separating the text from the tables, and is now better than ever.

*Dutton's Navigation & Piloting* is published by the Naval Institute Press, Annapolis, Maryland, and is now in its 13th Edition. Originally written by Commander Benjamin Dutton, U.S.N., in 1926, the volume achieved widespread recognition as the teaching text for the U.S. Naval Academy for many years. Like Bowditch, *Dut-*

*ton's Navigation & Piloting* is encyclopedic in scope and a fine reference volume.

Before leaving the subject of reference material, I should point out something often overlooked: there are usually excellent explanation sections in all the government publications. If you ever need a refresher in the use of a particular volume, or are seeking information beyond the scope of this book, try them as a source.

It's one thing to accumulate your charts and publications and another to stow them on board. First, with regard to charts, since they are your single most essential source of information, they deserve commensurate treatment. Take with you every chart you might expect to use on the voyage at hand and, unless you have extensive storage facilities aboard, consider leaving the surplus in a good place at home. Some navigators divide their charts into portfolios by areas and only take the applicable portfolios with them. On board, I find it best to fold the conventional charts in four parts, with the printed side out. I can then work in a space about 18 by 24 inches and the chart is ready for service without a lot of refolding. I recommend stowing the charts flat and in numerical order, and if you can't remember all the numbers, just keep one of the catalog folders handy. Above all, don't roll your charts except for shipping or you will constantly be fighting unruly paper instead of concentrating on your navigation.

As to publications, many of the same remarks apply. If you are short of space, leave the planning and reference volumes at home and take with you those pertaining to the cruise at hand. Since the combined weight of Bowditch and Dutton is thirteen pounds, and since at sea you will be actively navigating rather than studying, I think the suggestion will be self-evident.

# 2. Aids to Navigation

Aids to Navigation ("Navaids") include all those external devices which are established to assist the navigator in the safe conduct of his voyage. They may be *visual,* such as lights, beacons and buoys; *audible,* such as fog signals, bells or gongs; or *electronic,* like radiobeacons and Loran. Often, more than one category is combined in a single aid. While there are a few privately maintained navaids, the vast majority in the United States and Canada are the responsibility of the respective governments. In the U.S., the Coast Guard is charged with the operation and maintenance of public navigational aids, the total number of which is now in the order of fifty thousand.

The Coast Guard *Light List,* mentioned in Chapter 1, is the "bible" of navaids in the United States and the navigator ought to be familiar with its format and content. Figure 2-1 shows an extract from this publication and, beneath it, an illustration of one of the structures described: No. 1172, Peck Ledge Light. You will find this

| (1) No. | (2) Name Characteristic | (3) Location Lat. N.   Long. W. | (4) Nominal Range | (5) Ht. above water | (6) Structure Ht. above ground    Daymark | (7) Remarks    Year |
|---|---|---|---|---|---|---|
| | **NORWALK EAST APPROACH** | | | | | |
| | —Buoy 2 ..................... | In 22 feet ..........   41 04.4    73 20.8 | .......... | .... | Red nun ..................... | Red reflector. |
| | —Buoy 4 ..................... | In 13 feet, marks southwest end of rock reef at Channel Rock. | .......... | .... | Red nun ..................... | Red reflector. |
| | —Bell Buoy 5 ................. | In 13 feet .......... | ........ | .... | Black .............. | |
| 1172 | PECK LEDGE LIGHT 7 .......... Fl. G., 4ˢ | In 7 feet, on south side of east entrance to Cockenoe Island Harbor. 41 04.6    73 22.1 | 7 | .... | SB on white conical tower, middle part brown, on black cylindrical pier. | Higher intensity beam toward Long Island Sound and Grassy Hammock Rocks.   1906–1933 |
| 1173 | GRASSY HAMMOCK LIGHT 8...... Fl. R., 4ˢ | On rocks, north side of channel. 41 04.6    73 23.0 | 5 | 26 | TR on skeleton tower ......... | 1901–1968 |
| | —Buoy 9 ..................... | In 8 feet, on point of shoal north of Betts Island. | .......... | .... | Black can ............... | Green reflector. |
| | —Buoy 11 .................... | In 8 feet, off end of shoal northeast of Raymond Rocks. | .......... | .... | Black can ................. | Green reflector. |

*Figure 2–1. Using the Light List—Peck Ledge Light is described in detail in the extracted data. Below is the physical appearance of the described structure.*

light, as well as the other aids listed in the excerpt, on the nautical chart reproduction in Figure 1-2, in the eastern approach to Norwalk Harbor.

Aids to Navigation are located for purposes of position finding, as marks to keep the navigator clear of dangers (as is the case with Peck Ledge Light), or to indicate routes as do the buoys marking the Entrance Channel through Sheffield Island Harbor in Figure 1-2. The rationale behind the positioning of an aid is almost always self-evident.

Bouys and beacons or daymarks, except when used singly to mark an isolated danger, are shaped, colored, numbered and deployed according to a prescribed system. That in the United States and Canada is known as a *lateral* system. The extracts of pages 22–24 of Chart No. 1, found in the Appendix, show how the system works. If you refer once again to Figure 1-2, you can see as an example how the rule, "red, right, returning," applies to the bouys and beacons marking the channel through Sheffield Island Harbor and the easterly approach through Cockenoe Harbor. Even the waters offshore adhere to the pattern with red, even-numbered buoys, like *Norwalk Harbor Lighted Gong Buoy 24A* and *Great Reef Nun Buoy 24B,* on the north side of Long Island Sound, while corresponding, odd-numbered, black marks are found on the opposite shore. Understand the buoyage system thoroughly; it's the coastwise navigator's most readily available source of guidance.

Floating buoys, as well as fixed beacons, may have lights whose identifying characteristics are indicated on the charts and, in detail, in the *Light List.* Their purpose, of course, is to aid navigation at night, discussed further in Chapter 7.

Beacons and buoys, or a combination of the two, may be used as ranges. The word "range" in navigational terminology can have several meanings. In one case it refers to a measurement of distance but, in the present sense, range denotes two objects in line. A range supplies the navigator alignment information, such as the centerline of an improved channel, or the safe route across an obstructed area, without reference to the compass direction. The usual channel range is established with the rear mark higher than the front one, and lights of narrow beam-width may be exhibited to enhance the usefulness in periods of low visibility. Any two objects in line create a range, and any two *charted* objects in line can also provide a useful line of position, without reference to the compass, as will be explained in Chapter 6.

The first category of *visual* aids comprises the major light structures located along the seacoast and at important harbor entrances. Of particular advantage to the navigator approaching from offshore, these structures may be identified by their light characteristics, shown on the chart and in the *Light List,* which are displayed both at night and in reduced visibility; by their physical appearance, described in the *Light List;* or by their fog or radiobeacon signals, also found in the *Light List.*

*Audible* aids are almost always combined with visual ones and are intended to assist in locating or identifying a particular mark in low visibility. On buoys, four types of sound apparatus are normally found: single-tone bells, four-toned gongs, whistles (sometimes called "groaners" by sailors to describe their sound), and electrically operated horns. The first three are activated by the motion of the waves, while the last is designed for locations where the wave action is minimal and the sound generation might otherwise be undependable.

On beacons at important locations, electrically operated horns or, occasionally, mechanical bells may be installed to signal their presence. These, too, are noted on the chart and in the *Light List.* The major light structures almost always have the sound devices of the greatest intensity to increase the limits of their usefulness.

Their signals may be produced by horns, sirens, whistles, mechanical bells or diaphones (often a two-toned sound) which are aimed, when practicable, in the most critical directions. The type of sound apparatus is shown on the chart as part of the legend identified with the structure, while the characteristic and time sequence is described in the *Light List* in the "Remarks" column, (7).

Radiobeacons supplement visual and audible aids and are by far the most widely used *electronic* aid to navigation available to the yachtsman. Most radiobeacons are located in conjunction with other navaids, in situations in which their primary utilization, position finding in low visibility, can be used to the greatest advantage. There are presently about two hundred stations in the U.S. system, with more to be added.

Radiobeacons are indicated on the chart by a small circle around the location and the abbreviation, "R Bn," often accompanied by the frequency and characteristic of the radio signal. Details of the characteristic may be found in the *Light List* in all cases, where there is also a comprehensive summary of the system and some of its operational limitations. Figure 2-2 shows the present coverage of the radiobeacon system for the Atlantic and Gulf Coasts. Similar charts for other areas appear in the respective *Light Lists.*

Loran (*LO*ng *RA*nge *N*avigation) is another *electronic* aid to navigation which, with the development of smaller and more economical receivers, is finding increasing acceptance among yachtsmen, although still modest in absolute numbers when compared with the hundreds of thousands of radio direction finding sets in use. The principle of Loran is to transmit from shore stations signals which are interpreted by the vessel's receiver as an identified line of position. A lattice of these lines is over-printed on the smaller scale charts to enable position finding by inspection. The Loran system

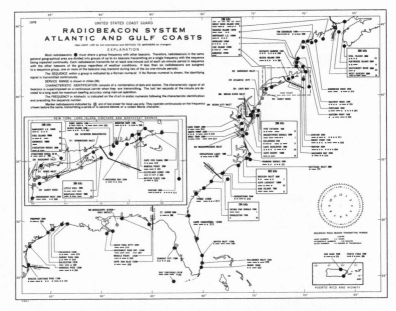

*Figure 2–2. Chartlet showing Radiobeacon System for the Atlantic and Gulf Coasts.*

is in a state of change, with the anticipated phasing out of the original, Loran-A network, and the expansion of the Loran-C system—a new version with improved coverage and accuracy—to meet the requirements of the coastwise navigator.

There are still other electronic devices serving as navaids, such as Omega, Decca, Sattelite systems and so forth, but the complexity, cost, and energy requirements are presently beyond the practical limits of most yachtsman navigating coastwise. Descriptions of these systems, for those who have the technical curiosity, may be found in both Bowditch and Dutton.

Radar (*RA*dio *D*etection *A*nd *R*anging) does not fit precisely our definition of aids to navigation with respect to being externally located. It is, on the other hand, interrelated with the navaid system in that many individual aids have radar reflectors or Racon (a transponder which returns a characteristic signal when triggered by the ship's radar). Although the equipment, its cost, space and energy requirements confine its use to larger yachts, radar does offer a superb navigation assist in periods of reduced visibility and when other methods are not practicable or available.

A note of caution, concerning *all* aids to navigation, involves blind reliance by newcomers to the boating scene. While the navaid system is remarkably reliable, the marine environment can be much more hostile than its counterpart ashore. As a consequence, the prudent navigator, even with the latest charts and publications aboard, is constantly on the alert for marks damaged, removed or displaced by storms, aids recently renumbered or relocated as part of a continuing improvement program or faulty light or sound characteristics due to the inevitable technical failures which happen occasionally, even in a system as well maintained as ours.

# 3. The Compass

One thing almost all navigators agree upon is that the single, most important instrument on board is the compass. While the concept of the magnetic compass dates back, perhaps, a thousand years, the modern ship's compass owes its lineage to Lord Kelvin's developments in the late nineteenth century. Today, all small-boat compasses are based on Kelvin's principles and, properly adjusted, they are instruments of remarkable accuracy and dependability. Your compass deserves your understanding and care. With both, it will be your unflagging guide across trackless waters.

Four main components of the marine compass are: *the binnacle,* the *bowl,* the *card* and the *lubber's line.* The binnacle is the base or stand in which the compass is housed and the bowl the body in which the card is mounted. The compass card is the movable, graduated part which indicates geographical direction, while the lubber's line serves as the index against which the card is read. In a portable, hand-bearing compass, the binnacle and bowl are combined in a convenient configuration for holding and a prism arrangement permits viewing the card and the objective over the lubber's line at the same time.

Compass cards are commonly graduated in degrees although a few, in the old, sailing-ship tradition, may also show the "point" system described in Chapter 1. For the purpose of our discussion, we'll deal strictly in degrees. Incidentally, in seagoing phraseology, the degrees in a compass direction are expressed as three numbers, adding zeros where necessary. Thus, 2° is spoken of as "zero-zero-two," 20° as "zero-two-zero," 200° as "two-zero-zero," and so forth around the 360-degree card. The identifiers "Compass," "Magnetic" or "True" are appended when needed to avoid ambiguity.

The compass, when used for steering, is read at the lubber's line which is aligned with the fore-and-aft axis of the vessel. The reading is called the "ship's heading." Bearings, which are the direction of one terrestrial point from another, can be taken by the steering compass either by aiming the lubber's line (and the ship's head) at the object or, somewhat less accurately but often more conveniently, by sighting the object across the center of the compass card while the vessel maintains its course.

The compass operates on the principle of aligning the magnets governing the card with the earth's magnetic field, with North on the card pointing to the North Magnetic Pole. It is often difficult to get neophyte helmsmen to realize that the ship's head, represented by the lubber's line, moves about the card which maintains a constant position with respect to North, and not the reverse.

Since the magnetic poles are some distance from the geographical poles and subject to a slow drift over a period of years, it follows that there will be a discrepancy between true North and the direction in which the compass points. This angular difference, together with any further divergence caused by the vessel's magnetism, add up to the so-called "compass error" which is considered to have two components: *variation* and *deviation.*

*Variation* is the difference between true and magnetic direction and is shown in the upper legend inside the compass rose on the chart for the particular locality (See Figure 1-2). The annual change is stated in the lower legend in the rose and is usually negligible if the chart is of recent date. The variation will change with the geographical location of the vessel and there is nothing the navigator can do about it except to note it accurately and apply it correctly.

*Deviation,* defined as the difference between the magnetic direction and the compass reading, is, on the other hand, a function of the vessel's magnetic field and it can be minimized by proper stowage of equipment and skillful compass adjustment. Certain ship's gear, such as the engine, is permanently fixed and its magnetic effect constant. Portable radios, flashlights, knives and the like sometimes find their way into the compass' magnetic field and cause temporary deviation which must be guarded against. A good rule is always to stow gear with magnetic properties in the same location as far from the compass as practicable, and to keep other movable magnetic articles away from the area of the compass when underway.

When more-or-less constant deviation exists, it can be minimized by using small correcting magnets, often located within the compass housing, to neutralize the vessel's magnetic effect. Most yachts with well designed compasses can reduce deviation to negligible terms, or to very small amounts, although probably not to zero. The process is called "adjusting" the compass and, properly, it should be carried out by a qualified professional.

In adjusting the compass on a small vessel, one typical procedure is to place the vessel on a northerly heading at a known location, reading at the same time the *compass* bearing of a distant, charted object or range ashore whose *magnetic* direction from the known location has been predetermined from the chart. The difference between the observed *compass* bearing and the predetermined *magnetic* bearing is the deviation on the North heading. Half that deviation is removed by adjusting the athwartship correcting magnet. The vessel is then headed East and the same process repeated, correcting half the error by the fore-and-aft adjustment. Next, the heading is altered to South and half the error remaining removed with the same corrector as for North. Finally, heading West, half the error found there is eliminated with the fore-and-aft adjustment. The routine is repeated several more times to obtain the minimum deviation.

The professional adjuster always rechecks the compass on a whole series of headings, a process known as "swinging ship," and then prepares a deviation table listing the deviation, if any, on each heading for the navigator's permanent reference. A typical deviation table might show a column for magnetic heading, a second column for the corresponding deviation and a third for compass heading so that corrections can be applied readily and without error when called for. Just remember that the amount of deviation is always a function of the ship's *heading* and not of the direction of a bearing line.

Good navigators make a habit of checking the compass carefully at the beginning of the season, after any changes have been made in the vessel or her stowage, or at the outset of a cruise. Less formal checks are also made along the way and this can be done by comparison with another compass of known accuracy—like a good hand-bearing compass—by steering on charted ranges or on fixed courses between points, by bearings of distant objects from known positions or, if you have a celestial navigator aboard, by the bearing or "azimuth" of the sun at a given moment.

Having talked about compass errors, what do we do about it? You have seen that the error is separated into two parts—*variation,* the difference between *true* and *magnetic* direction, and *deviation,* the difference between *magnetic* and *compass.*

A classic sailor's trick for remembering this relationship is the phrase,

| "Can | Dead | Men | Vote | Twice." |
|-------|------|-----|------|---------|
| o     | e    | a   | a    | r       |
| m     | v    | g   | r    | u       |
| p     | i    | n   | i    | e       |
| a     | a    | e   | a    |         |
| s     | t    | t   | t    |         |
| s     | i    | i   | i    |         |
|       | o    | c   | o    |         |
|       | n    |     | n    |         |

Since going from *compass* to *true* represents decreasing error, the process is called "correcting" and the rule in going from one classification to the next is "correcting, add easterly." The opposite way, from *true* to *compass,* is called "uncorrecting" and the rule is the reverse, "uncorrecting, add westerly." You need to know whether the variation and deviation are East or West (if it is not already indicated on your chart or deviation card) and the rule here is, if *magnetic* reads less than *true,* the variation is East—"East reads least"—and the same applies to deviation if *compass* reads less than *magnetic.*

As a practical example, a *compass* heading of 212°, corrected for 3° easterly deviation, becomes a *magnetic* heading of 215°. Applying a westerly variation of 15°, the *true* heading is 200°. You could also have taken the net of the 3° E deviation and the 15° W variation, making a 12° W total compass error, and applied that to your 212° *compass* heading to arrive at 200° *True.*

Going in the opposite way, if your charted course is

200° *True* and your variation is 15° W, the variation is *added* to the *true* course to yield the *magnetic* course of 215°. Then, if the deviation is 3° E, the *magnetic* course is *uncorrected* by *subtracting* the easterly deviation, and the instructions are given to the helmsman to steer 212° by the *compass.* Fortunate is the navigator with negligible deviation, as he has only to apply variation with the proper sign when going back and forth between *compass* (the same as *magnetic* in that case) and *true.*

In practice, the navigator plots his course on the chart, converts it to the proper compass heading, and gives instructions to the helmsman. The prudent navigator, however, checks after steadying on the new course to make certain that the helmsman is steering the proper course, that its relationship to the geographical situation and nearby navaids is reasonable, and that the compass corrections have been applied in the right way. Human errors are often more significant than compass errors, and overlooking this fact can prove embarrassing to say the least.

# 4. Onboard Equipment for Coastwise Navigation

In addition to the appropriate charts and publications and a reliable steering compass, you will want certain other equipment and instrumentation aboard to practice effective coastwise navigation. For convenience, we can consider these in four groups: plotting instruments, measuring instruments, positioning devices and communication equipment. The applicable operating techniques will be discussed in the chapters to follow.

For establishing distances, courses and bearings on your chart, you need a pair of dividers for distance measurement and a protractor or equivalent device to measure angles. Dividers come in a variety of types, two of which, commonly found aboard yachts, are shown in Figure 4-1. The draftsman's dividers are preferred by most professional navigators and, with a little practice, can be manipulated nicely with one hand. The second variety, sometimes called "yachtsman's" or "one-hand" dividers," has a number of adherents among small-boat navigators. Usually constructed of solid brass, this type

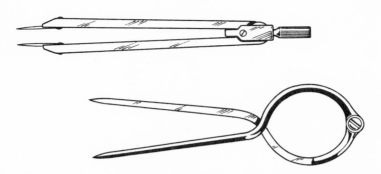

*Figure 4–1. Two types of dividers commonly used by yachtsmen—Draftsman's Dividers (top) and Yachtsman's Dividers (bottom).*

has the advantage of being able to withstand a little rougher treatment and is possibly a bit easier for the beginner to learn to work. On balance, however, a good pair of standard, six- or seven-inch draftsman's dividers are hard to beat. Dividers, one leg of which contains a marking device, are called compasses. This is a useful tool for scribing circles, plotting the range of visibility of a light and so forth, but a cheap pair like those used in a secondary school math class is really all you need.

Strictly speaking, a *protractor* is a scale for measuring angles, while *plotters* are devices for measuring and plotting courses and bearings on charts. In the yachting vernacular, however, the two terms are often used interchangeably to describe the usual plotting tool. While small-boat navigators can agree universally on the importance of a good steering compass, there are almost as many opinions as there are navigators as to the selection of the best plotting instrument.

Plotters can be separated into two major categories: those which require reference to the compass rose on the chart, and those which require reference only to parallels of latitude or meridians of longitude. In the first group are found such devices as parallel rules which are used to transfer direction from one part of the chart to the compass rose or back again. A similar result can be achieved by the use of two similar, right triangles or a transparent sheet of plastic with parallel lines ruled upon it. A feature of this class of plotter is that reference can be made to either the magnetic or true compass rose, thereby eliminating the correction for variation.

The second group of plotters, combining a protractor with a straight-edge, can be subdivided into two categories, *fixed* and *movable*. A typical example of the *fixed* variety is the USPS Course Plotter or the common, aircraft plotter from which this type evolved. In using these, the straight-edge is aligned with the course or bearing, the bullseye centered over any convenient meridian or parallel, and the true direction read at the intersection of that line with the applicable protractor scale. The handy size, the absence of moving parts and the feature of not having to refer to the compass rose (which might not appear on the open section of a folded chart), make this type of plotter popular with a number of small-boat navigators.

Protractors combined with *movable* straight-edges, pivoted at the center of the arc, are sometimes called "one-arm protractors." They are particularly suitable for coastwise navigation. In use, the straight-edge is aligned with the course or bearing and the circular protractor is rotated to line up with the parallels and meridians on the chart. The true direction is then read at the index. Although the mental arithmetic in converting true to magnetic and vice versa is not very taxing, some instruments of this type have supplementary scales to allow for variation and to permit direct magnetic readings. Figure 4-2 shows examples of parallel rules, a fixed course plotter, and a one-arm protractor, all typical of the instruments found on small boats.

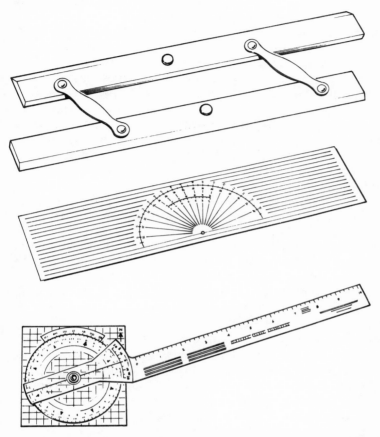

*Figure 4–2. Plotting Tools commonly used by yachts-men—Parallel Rules, Fixed Course Plotter, One-Arm Protractor.*

The ultimate plotting device is the Universal Drafting Machine, a standard engineering draftsman's tool ashore, which is used widely on Navy and Merchant ships. The drafting machine does require space to set it up and operate it, and some care to maintain it at sea. Adaptations more suitable to the yachting environment are available and occasionally seen aboard but the single-arm protractor types appear to predominate. My best advice is to select a type easy for you to understand and work, and to practice with it under all conditions until its operation becomes second nature. And when plotting with any device, don't forget sharp pencils. The hallmark of a professional navigator is the neatness and precision of his plot.

"Lead, log and lookout" were the bywords of the ancient mariner, and the information they convey is no less important to small-boat navigating today. The measuring instruments now available may be a far cry from those of the ancients, but the utilization of their data follows time-honored patterns.

Traditionally, depth was measured by a marked lead line, often "armed" with tallow to sample the quality of the bottom. It is still the most direct and foolproof way of determining the depth beneath your boat, especially in the shallow inland passages frequented by yachts. Many small-boat navigators keep a hand lead line aboard, if only for back-up. Today, however, is the electronic age and there are many excellent, economical instruments available. The specific configuration of your model, be it digital or with flashing-light display, indicating or recording, is a subjective choice. Most important is the selection of an instrument which will give you accurate results and dependable service, since a good depth finder is probably the most valuable device, aside from the compass, aboard most small boats.

The speed of a vessel through the water and, by the application of time, the distance traveled, is another vital bit of intelligence the navigator needs. This was originally measured by a "log"—a floating object thrown overboard from the forward part of the ship and timed to pass a measured distance alongside. Four hundred years or so ago, someone had the bright idea of attaching a line to the object which could then be paid out and measured. Eventually the line was knotted at predetermined intervals so that the number of knots paid out in a given time was indicative of the ship's speed. Not only is this the origin of "log," but also of "knot" which has come to mean a speed of one nautical mile per hour. Incidentally, you never say "knots per hour" unless you are talking about an acceleration rate. The expression is redundant and " 'lubberly."

Today there is a wide variety of mechanical and electronic devices for measuring both speed through the water and distance traveled with much greater accuracy than was ever possible with the old-fashioned log. Again, the choice is highly subjective though the need for the information, especially when navigating coastwise, remains undiminished. A device measuring only speed or distance is often used in conjunction with a stopwatch to determine the other value. That same stopwatch may also prove useful for timing the sequence of lighted navaids or fog signals, or for "running your time" when navigating in the fog as explained in Chapter 7.

The "lookout" portion of the mariner's credo involves not only visual observation—the most important safety device on the ship—but also the measurement of the elements necessary for position finding. In the first case, binoculars are an invaluable aid to the lookout. Probably best suited to small-boat navigation and representing an excellent compromise between magnifying power, size of field, light-gathering ability and weight and bulk is the 7 × 50 size—standard for deck officers in the Navy. Binoculars, or "glasses" in nautical parlance, are particularly useful in spotting and identifying, at a safe distance, aids to navigation, objects ashore and the intentions of approaching vessels. The light-gathering power of the 7 × 50 glass is extremely helpful in sorting things out at twilight, and even in night piloting. Some navigators have a personal pair of binoculars, adjusted to their own eyesight, and kept separate for instant use when required.

For determining direction, as we have discussed in Chapter 3, you have the ship's compass to steer by and bearings can be measured across it if it is suitably located. It is often more convenient to have a second, hand-bearing compass aboard which permits independent and direct measurement of bearings and also serves as a check on the steering compass.

The distance from an object observed at sea can be measured by such devices as optical range finders, stadimeters or the navigator's sextant when the object is visible, and by radar, which can "see" and measure the range as well as the bearing during restricted visibility. While not essential instruments in the sense the compass and depth finder are, distance measuring devices do provide useful information to the navigator, being of particular value in positioning.

As to positioning devices, today's yachtsman is again the beneficiary of the electronic age. Some small vessels are fitted with radar, a device developed in World War II which emits a short burst of electrical energy through a highly directional antenna and, by measuring the time lapse until the signal "bounces" back to the receiver and noting the position of the rotating antenna, translates its result into the range (distance) and bearing (direction) of the target. While often installed for its primary utility in collision avoidance, radar, for those yachtsmen who can accommodate the installation, is a superb tool for positioning in the close confines of coastal waters.

Radio direction finders, while lacking the precision of radar, are by far the most widely used radio aid to navigation because the equipment is readily available, is modestly priced, small and self-contained and, subject to understanding its limitations, uncomplicated to use and adequate to the yachtsman's needs except, perhaps, in the most severely restricted waters. RDF works by means of a characteristic signal transmitted on the low frequency radio band from a charted location. A shipboard radio receiver is used to identify the station and, by rotating a directional antenna to the null (minimum signal) point, the bearing of that station can be determined and a line of position laid down on the chart.

There are two general types of radio direction finding apparatus in common use on small boats. The first has a rotating antenna, integral with the set, with an index which is aligned with the vessel's fore-and-aft line. The navigator tunes the receiver to the appropriate station, rotates the antenna to the null, and reads the *relative* bearing (the bearing relative to the ship's head) at the index. The vessel's course at the moment the reading is made is applied to the relative bearing to arrive at the compass bearing for plotting.

The second type of RDF consists of a separate, hand-held antenna with a magnetic compass attached. Used in the manner of a hand-bearing compass, when the null is found, the compass bearing can be read out directly, assuring quicker, and generally more accurate results. Bearing accuracy of the order of ± 3° is reasonable to expect with a good set and an accomplished operator. If you do intend to use RDF, however, you should be familiar with its idiosyncrasies and limitations—there is an excellent summary in the Introduction to the *Light List*—and practice with your set under favorable conditions until you attain the desired proficiency.

Loran, mentioned in Chapter 2, is a modern, electronic aid to navigation which, by means of a special receiver, enables radio signals from shore stations to be translated into charted position lines of great accuracy. The Government's decision to expand the Loran-C system, making it the preferred system in the so-called Coastal Confluence Zone, has provided the impetus to a number of manufacturers to develop Loran sets with the small-boat navigator's requirements in mind. As the coverage improves and the equipment cost is reduced, there is little doubt that Loran will become a widely used positioning device for yachtsmen engaged in coastwise navigation as well as offshore.

We mentioned earlier the use of the sextant for distance determination. The same instrument can be used horizontally for obtaining a position line from the difference in bearing between two charted objects, or for obtaining an actual fix from three such points. The procedures are described in Chapter 6. In this mode, the sextant, in conjunction with a special plotting instrument called a "three-arm protractor," can rightfully be included in the list of onboard positioning devices for coastwise work.

The final equipment group comprises communication devices which, while not immediately involved in the navigation procedure, do supply the navigator with information contributing to the safe conduct of his voyage. The navigator today relies on his radio for such things as weather reports, notices of dangers to navigation, time signals, inlet conditions, bridge opening communication and, if in distress, for timely assistance.

Onboard equipment is only useful if it is available when needed, if it works properly when required and is understood by the operator. While this may seem obvious, it is all too often the opposite one finds on a small boat. The moral is to be careful in the selection of the gear you really need and will use, see to its proper stowage and maintenance aboard and learn to use it *before* your life depends on it. That is *your* responsibility.

# 5. Dead Reckoning

There has always been interesting speculation about the true origin of the term, "dead reckoning." Bowditch concludes that the expression stems from the first use of the log which, relative to the vessel's movement, was *dead* in the water. Other historians maintain that it is merely a shortened form of "deduced reckoning"—the estimating of the vessel's true track after taking into account the effects of wind and current.

Regardless of the version you prefer, dead reckoning in modern navigation is simply the process of locating your position by applying courses and distances travelled from your last known position. The point so determined is called the "Dead Reckoning Position," or DR. If sailing through a current of *known* direction and velocity, its effect may also be taken into account in reckoning your position although such a determination is more correctly called an "Estimated Position" (EP).

The vast majority of navigators derive their dead reckoning positions graphically, that is, by plotting each successive course and distance on the chart. The outstanding advantage of this method in coastal waters is that it enables the navigator to visualize the relationship between his vessel's track and marks or hazards along the course. It is possible to locate a DR position mathematically by "traverse sailing"—a technique which will be described later in this chapter—but its practical value is limited except in special circumstances.

We have seen in Chapter 1 that the Mercator projection used in modern charts is particularly well suited to plotting since the course line can be drawn as a straight line crossing all the meridians at the same angle, and distances can be determined readily from the latitude scale. In practice, the navigator simply lays out his course from a departure or turning point by means of his protractor, and steps off the appropriate distance with his dividers.

Careful navigation requires careful plotting which includes neat and accurate labeling of the plot. Customarily, courses are indicated above the track and are expressed as three digits after the prefix, "C." Zeros are added where necessary so, for example, 45° becomes "045," just the way it is properly spoken. Speeds are indicated below the course line, following the prefix, "S." Unless otherwise marked (using the suffix, "M," for instance, to designate a magnetic course), courses and bearings are assumed to be *true* and speeds to be in knots. Times are expressed in four digits using the 24-hour clock, thus, 2:48 P.M. becomes "1448," and 4:00 A.M., "0400."

Figure 5-1 shows a typically labeled DR plot in which the course is 116° Magnetic, the speed 6 knots, and the DR position indicated at 12 minutes after noon. Some navigators prefer a half circle at the DR or to run the legend diagonally to avoid possible confusion with a fix —an EP is sometimes marked with a small square for the same purpose. Most important, however, is labeling the plot clearly, consistently and promptly. It will return

*Figure 5–1. Label-*
*ing the plot—*
*Course is shown* 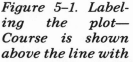 **1210 DR**
*above the line with*
*appropriate prefix and suffix and speed below. The*
*Dead Reckoning position is labeled with the time.*

you good dividends in eliminating confusion and error.

To review this essential technique, let's look at a practical example which you can follow on the chart reproduction in Figure 5-2. The navigator departs from his
favorite fishing ground at the western end of a four-
fathom bank just south of the Norwalk Islands. His
depth finder confirmed his location over a 27-foot spot.
Getting underway at noon, the navigator set his course
at 116° Magnetic and plotted it on the chart. The vessel's
speed, measured by log, was 6.0 knots and, after ten
minutes of steaming, the distance run was calculated to
be exactly one nautical mile. (Most such calculations
can be performed mentally, but a slide-rule device or
calculator can be used if preferred.) The distance run
was stepped off along the course line by the dividers
which had been set at one mile—one minute of latitude
on the latitude scale. The DR position at 1210 was then
labeled on the plot.

The navigator next changed course to 84° Magnetic
and reduced speed to 5 knots. Running on this course for
six minutes, he plotted the new track and stepped off the
half-mile he calculated he had traveled during the period. This point became his 1216 DR.

Altering course once more, this time to 13° Magnetic,
and maintaining his 5-knot speed, the navigator headed
for his rendezvous in the vicinity of Gong Buoy "24A."
At 1223, the depth finder indicated that the vessel had

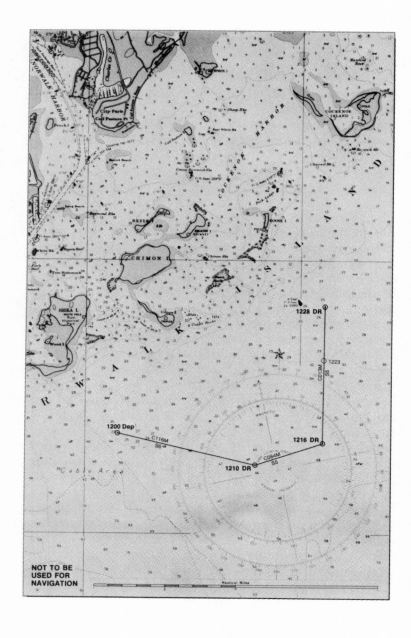

NOT TO BE
USED FOR
NAVIGATION

crossed the five-fathom (30-foot) curve, confirming the approximate DR position at that time.

At 1228, the navigator reckoned he had covered a mile on his final leg and so marked his 1228 DR on the chart. Seeing the Gong Buoy off his port beam, he then knew his 1228 DR was approximately correct.

In this example, you will notice that the navigator used magnetic courses on his plot—the most common practice on yachts. He could have translated the magnetic directions to true, either by reference to the magnetic rose, had he been plotting by that method, or by applying variation as we learned in Chapter 3. Either way, the plot would have looked exactly the same except for the course labeling.

The water you sail through—and this is particularly true where tidal conditions exist—is itself in constant motion. This has the effect of altering the speed or direction actually made good over the bottom and introduces a corresponding error in the dead reckoning position. The DR position, therefore, must always be considered as inexact, surrounded, if you wish, by an "area of uncertainty." Since the effect of current is proportional to time, it follows that the greater the time elapsed since the last fix, the greater the area of uncertainty about the DR becomes.

All diverting influences are lumped together as "current" and if the direction toward which it flows (the "set") and the rate of that flow (the "drift") are known, an improved estimate of your position can be derived by applying these factors to your DR. With practice, an observant navigator can make a fair estimate of the set and drift of a current by noticing such things as the flow of water around buoys or anchored boats, the divergence from his course as seen from leading marks,

*Figure 5–2. A typical plot of a Dead Reckoning Track from Departure at 1200 to Arrival at 1228.*

ranges or back bearings (bearings on objects astern), or from the measured difference between the DR and the actual position after sailing a segment of the course. The *Tidal Current Tables,* explained in Chapter 1, also present, or permit the calculation of, set and drift data for a number of locations. Learning to estimate and reckon with the current is a technique that predicted loggers have developed to a fine art.

There are three cases in "current sailing" in which you will be interested. The first, illustrated graphically in Figure 5-3, is that in which the course you have steered, your speed through the water and the set and drift of the current are all known quantities. You want to know your most probable position or, more frequently, the course you actually made good over the bottom and the actual speed along that track.

Referring to Figure 5-3, *A* represents the point of departure, the line from *A* to *B* the course steered, and the length of side *AB* the speed through the water. Without current, point *B* would be the DR position after one hour of elapsed time. But the current did exist, represented by the side *BC* whose direction is the set and whose length is the drift. By constructing a line from *B* (the DR position), we arrive at *C* which is our correct position. This corrected position is called the "Estimated Posi-

*Figure 5–3. Vector Diagram for finding Course and Speed Made Good through a known current.*

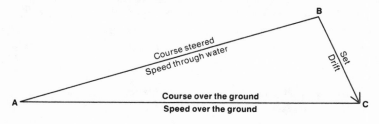

tion," or EP, and may be vital to know if you are navigating in dangerous waters. The side *AC* represents by its direction the actual course made good and, by its length, the corresponding speed made good.

The sides of the current triangle used in this way are called "vectors," which are simply straight lines which represent direction by their orientation, and magnitude by their length. You can construct a current triangle right on your plot, and it is recommended that you do so when you are in pilot waters and the current data are known or can be accurately estimated.

A second current sailing case arises when you know the course you want to make good and the speed through the water that you expect to sail. Then, knowing the set and drift of the current, you want to determine the course to steer and to find the actual speed you will make good over the intended track. Figure 5-4 illustrates the geometry of that situation but the solution is a little trickier than the first case. Perhaps the easiest way is to construct a current triangle on any convenient compass rose as illustrated in Figure 5-5. The steps in this procedure which you can follow in the figure are:

1.  Lay out the course to be made good (COG) from

*Figure 5–4. Vector Diagram for finding Course to Steer through a known current and resulting Speed Made Good.*

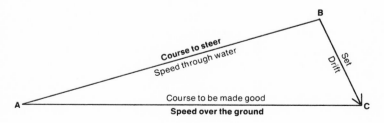

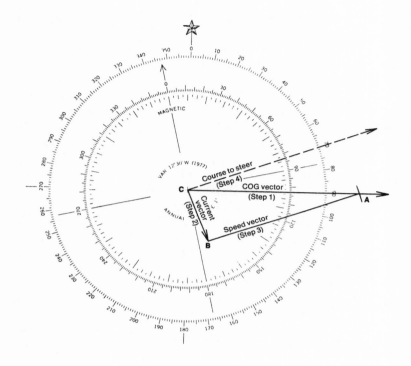

*Figure 5-5. Constructing a Current Diagram on a compass rose—Plotting the COG, Current and Speed Vectors produces the Course to Steer and the Speed Made Good.*

the center of the rose, *C,* of indefinite length. This we'll call the "COG Vector."

2.  Draw a line from the center of the rose, *C,* in the direction of the current's set, and of a length representative of the drift. Any convenient scale can be selected for this line, *CB,* the "Current Vector."

3.  Using the same scale, set the dividers for your

speed through the water. With one point at the end of the Current Vector, *B,* swing an arc and determine the point, *A,* of intersection of this "Speed Vector" with the COG Vector. The resulting length of the COG Vector from the center of the rose to the intersection, line *CA,* measured at the selected scale, represents the speed which will be made good over the intended track.

4. The direction of the Speed Vector, line *BA,* is the course to steer. This can be found right on the rose by drawing a line parallel to the Speed Vector, *BA,* through the center, *C,* of the compass rose.

On occasion, the navigator may need to specify *both* the course and speed to be made good, and wants to know the course to steer and the speed required through the water to accomplish his objective. This solution is as simple as the first and quite similar. A line is constructed in the direction of the intended track, its length representing the desired speed over that track. From the starting point, draw a second vector in the direction of the set, its length representing the drift. The direction of the line connecting the ends of the two vectors is the course to steer, and its length the speed you must make through the water.

The mathematical name for the procedure we have just been following is "vector arithmetic." While we chose to solve the current sailing problems by a practical, graphic method, it is perfectly possible to perform the task by math alone. The principle is to translate each vector into its equivalent dimensions in a North-South and an East-West direction. For example, a course of 090 at 10 knots is the equivalent of zero knots in a North-South direction and 10 knots in an East-West direction. A course of 053 at 5 knots is the equivalent of 3 knots N-S and 4 knots E-W. You can prove this graphically. The process involved is simply changing the direction and magnitude from the "polar" coordinates you are used to working with in courses and distances on a chart to the equivalent "rectangular" (N-S and E-W) coordinates.

In dead reckoning, such an exercise is seldom of more than historic interest since the excellence of modern charts makes the graphic solution much more practical. Under certain special circumstances, however, as in a sailboat tacking to windward on a large number of short courses, a mathematical solution of the DR might be preferred to the rather voluminous chart work involved. Similarly, in lifeboat navigation, where there might not be a chart available, the vector arithmetic solution, called "traverse sailing" can be useful.

As a practical example of traverse sailing, look at Figure 5-6. The three legs, *AB, BC* and *CD* are those sailed in our earlier dead reckoning exercise (Figure 5-2). Supposing you wanted to know the direct course and distance from *A* to *D*? One way to determine it, and an easy one at that, is to measure it on your plot. The mathematical alternative is to transform each of the courses and distances into their rectangular coordinate equivalents, find the algebraic sum of each of the two components, and transform that back to a single course and distance in the "polar" system. That exercise can be performed quite handily on a calculator that has the capability or with a traverse table such as Bowditch, Table 3. Try it yourself; the answer is: Course 070, and Distance 1.7 miles.

In the same problem, if the latitude and longitude of the point of departure are known and you wish to find those at the destination, the N-S component can be determined and applied directly to the latitude (since a minute of latitude is everywhere the equivalent of a nautical mile). Longitude, on the other hand, is a bit trickier. You will have determined the net mileage of the E-W component but, since the length of a minute of longitude gets smaller as the meridians converge to-

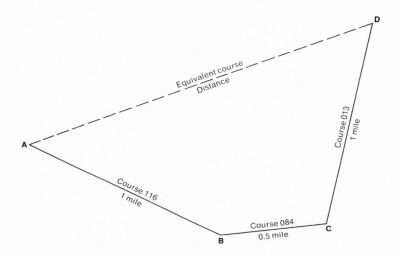

*Figure 5–6. Traverse Sailing—The algebraic sum of the vectors AB, BC, and CD is equivalent to the direct Course and Distance, vector AD.*

wards the poles, it is necessary to apply a factor dependent on your latitude to transform the miles into minutes of longitude. This can be done by computation or, more easily, by Bowditch, Table 3. After experimenting with the procedure, however, I think you'll agree that in most circumstances the graphic solution is far simpler.

Dead reckoning, in the final analysis, is only a process of positioning yourself by keeping track of where and how far you have come from a known starting point. While your DR position can seldom be expected to be exact, it can be as good as the information you apply to it. Consequently, you will want to gain all the experience you can, not only in the techniques of reckoning and plotting, but also in learning to judge the accuracy of your work with confidence. That is still the *art* in the *science* of navigation.

# 6. Position Finding

Although his vessel's probable position has been established by dead reckoning, the navigator should seek every opportunity to confirm or correct that position by an independent "fix," determined without reference to a previous position and, most frequently, derived from the intersection of two or more lines of position. The process is called "piloting" and is described by Bowditch as "navigation involving frequent or continuous determination of position or a line of position relative to geographical points, to a high degree of accuracy."

Notice the emphasis on "lines of position," a most important concept and one that you should understand thoroughly. A line of position is a line determined by observation or measurement, on some point of which a vessel is located. Lines of position can be obtained in a variety of ways although bearings on fixed objects are probably used most frequently. As in dead reckoning, some solutions can be derived mathematically, but here again, the graphic solution by plotting on the chart is usually the most practical. In inshore waters it is also the safest method since it indicates clearly the vessel's proximity to navigational hazards along its course and, properly plotted and labeled, the graphic presentation helps avoid the potential confusion in a fast-moving, complicated piloting exercise.

Bearings, we have seen, can be taken either by observation across the steering compass or, more conveniently, by a hand-bearing compass. Bearings are measured clockwise from a reference direction through 360 degrees. For bearings taken with a compass, the reference direction is North—usually *Magnetic* North since magnetic compasses are almost universal on small boats. It is possible, though more cumbersome and usually less accurate, to take *relative* bearings which use the ship's head as the reference direction. The compass bearing is then obtained by applying the relative bearing to the vessel's heading as indicated by the steering compass, at the moment of measurement.

In Figure 6-1, an observer is shown taking bearings of two charted objects, a lighthouse and a prominent house ashore. It so happened that he also had two conveniently located harbor buoys he could line up as ranges in each case which gave him a double-check on his bearings. Notice that the "spread" between the two bearing lines is close to the ideal right angle, thus minimizing the position error resulting from small errors in taking or plotting the bearings. It is generally recommended to avoid fixes using position lines which intersect at less than 30 degrees, *unless no better lines are available.*

Having taken the bearings, the navigator plots them on the chart using the same tools and techniques as he did in his dead reckoning plot. The line of position, or the useful portion of it near the vessel's location, is drawn from the charted object in the direction *opposite* to the bearing—the "reciprocal bearing." The reason for

*Figure 6–1. Observer taking bearings of terrestrial objects with a hand-bearing compass.*

this is obvious since the bearing is *taken* from seaward but *plotted* from the object.

Figure 6-2 shows the navigator's plot of the bearings taken in Figure 6-1. The navigator elected, in this case, to plot in true direction but, as explained earlier, he could equally well have used magnetic and only the labeling would have been different. The first bearing, 312°, was plotted from the lighthouse in the reciprocal direction, 132° and, in keeping with convention, labeled with the time and bearing as taken. Note that the practice of labeling bearing lines calls for the time above the

*Figure 6–2. A Fix plotted from two intersecting lines of postion.*

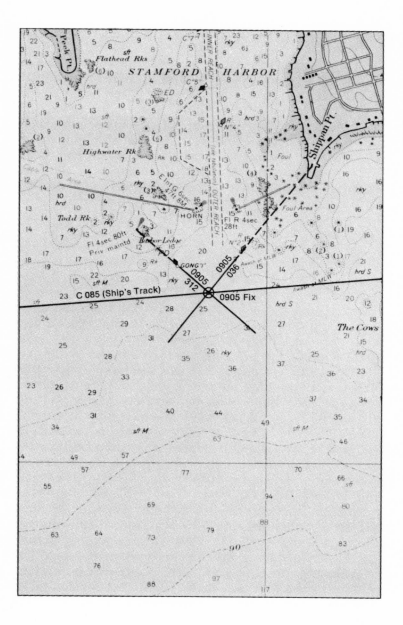

line and the direction from seaward below it. While all of our examples are so labeled, if there is no possibility of confusion as to the time of observation or the source and direction of the position line, some navigators choose, as a practical matter, to leave out either or both labels in order to keep the plot uncluttered. Since the fix in Figure 6-2 is clearly the result of simultaneous bearings on two obvious objects taken at 9:05 A.M., the position line labels might have been omitted in this instance without detracting from the plot. The best rule, however, is always to label if there is any possibility of future question.

Besides visual compass bearings of terrestrial objects, there are a number of other ways to obtain lines of position. In Figure 6-2, for example, the navigator, having aligned the gong buoy with the lighthouse, created a "range," and a line through both objects on the chart could be plotted without requiring the actual compass direction—although in this case it did provide a convenient double-check. A range can be created by any two charted features in line, such as a fixed navigational aid in line with the high point of an island. In many places fixed navaids have been deliberately placed, as discussed in Chapter 2, to provide the navigator alignment information in critical areas. Lines established by these ranges are simply another form of position line and the navigator who is constantly thinking in these terms is conscious of every opportunity for a "free" line of position from a range.

Position lines can be obtained electronically by radio direction finder bearings—taking care in interpreting their accuracy—or Loran lines or radar bearings which are highly accurate in a properly operating set. The technique of obtaining a line of position from a given apparatus is a function of the particular device and its operating instructions. The procedure for utilizing it is the same as for any other line obtained visually or by celestial navigation. A word of caution is in order, however, as even the finest electronic devices are capable of malfunctioning occasionally in the hostile environment of a small boat at sea, and the navigator who is not thoroughly familiar with conventional practices may find himself in an embarrassing situation if he relies totally upon electronics.

Another type of position line is one derived from a "distance-off" measurement. Such a line is actually the circumference of a circle whose radius is the distance from the object. It is plotted with compasses, placing one point on the charted object and scribing the appropriate portion of the arc in the area in which the vessel is presumed to be located. If a bearing and a distance-off can be obtained on the same object simultaneously (radar does just this, but you can do it visually, too), you have in effect two intersecting lines of position and, by definition, a fix. Figure 6-3 illustrates a case in which the range, *D,* from a conspicuous flagpole was measured at 10:30 a.m. at 2.1 miles. At the same time, the bearing was found to be 075° True. Where the two lines of position cross is the 1030 Fix.

Besides radar ranging, there are several ways to measure distance-off visually, requiring one form or another of optical instrument. Most frequently found aboard small boats are optical rangefinders which measure distance, the way your eyes do, by the angle of convergence between the lines of sight to an object from two, separated lenses; and sextants, which measure the angular height of an object, or width of a baseline, of known dimension. Stadimeters, which operate similarly to a sextant, are common on Naval vessels but are not often seen on yachts. Small, hand-held rangefinders are most accurate for short distances (50 to 1000 yards), while sextants are practical from a half to several miles, depending on the dimension of the object or baseline measured.

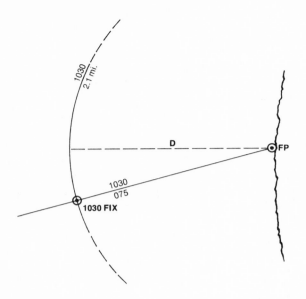

*Figure 6–3. A line of position from a distance-off measurement is the circumference of a circle whose radius, D, is the distance-off. The intersection with a line of position from a simultaneous bearing produces a fix.*

Used in the conventional, vertical position, the sextant measures an angle by bringing the top of an observed object to the visible horizon or, to the object's waterline if it is within the horizon. The navigator must correct the reading for the index error of the sextant, if any, and for the height of eye above the water at the time of observation. The correction for height of eye, called the "Dip" (D), may be found in the Dip table in the *Nautical Almanac,* or in Bowditch, which is reproduced in Figure 6-4. Alternatively, the D correction can be determined by the formula: Dip, in minutes = 0.97 $\sqrt{\text{height of eye, in feet}}$. The Dip correction is always negative. Thus, for a height of eye of 9 feet, D is −2.9′.

*Figure 6–4. The Dip Table from the Nautical Almanac— The correction to the sextant reading for all heights of eye between 8.6 and 9.2 feet is −2.9'.*

**DIP**

| Ht. of Eye | Corrn | Ht. of Eye | Ht. of Eye | Corrn |
|---|---|---|---|---|
| m | | ft. | m | |
| 2·4 | −2·8 | 8·0 | 1·0 — 1·8 | |
| 2·6 | −2·9 | 8·6 | 1·5 — 2·2 | |
| 2·8 | −3·0 | 9·2 | 2·0 — 2·5 | |
| 3·0 | −3·1 | 9·8 | 2·5 — 2·8 | |
| 3·2 | −3·2 | 10·5 | 3·0 — 3·0 | |
| 3·4 | −3·3 | 11·2 | See table | |
| 3·6 | −3·4 | 11·9 | ← | |
| 3·8 | −3·5 | 12·6 | m | |
| 4·0 | −3·6 | 13·3 | 20 — 7·9 | |
| 4·3 | −3·7 | 14·1 | 22 — 8·3 | |
| 4·5 | −3·8 | 14·9 | 24 — 8·6 | |
| 4·7 | −3·9 | 15·7 | 26 — 9·0 | |
| 5·0 | −4·0 | 16·5 | 28 — 9·3 | |
| 5·2 | −4·1 | 17·4 | | |
| 5·5 | −4·2 | 18·3 | 30 — 9·6 | |
| 5·8 | −4·3 | 19·1 | 32 — 10·0 | |
| 6·1 | −4·4 | 20·1 | 34 — 10·3 | |
| 6·3 | −4·5 | 21·0 | 36 — 10·6 | |
| 6·6 | −4·6 | 22·0 | 38 — 10·8 | |
| 6·9 | −4·7 | 22·9 | | |
| 7·2 | −4·8 | 23·9 | 40 — 11·1 | |
| 7·5 | −4·9 | 24·9 | 42 — 11·4 | |
| 7·9 | −5·0 | 26·0 | 44 — 11·7 | |
| 8·2 | −5·1 | 27·1 | 46 — 11·9 | |
| 8·5 | −5·2 | 28·1 | 48 — 12·2 | |
| 8·8 | −5·3 | 29·2 | ft. | |
| 9·2 | −5·4 | 30·4 | 2 — 1·4 | |
| 9·5 | −5·5 | 31·5 | 4 — 1·9 | |
| 9·9 | −5·6 | 32·7 | 6 — 2·4 | |
| 10·3 | −5·7 | 33·9 | 8 — 2·7 | |
| 10·6 | −5·8 | 35·1 | 10 — 3·1 | |
| 11·0 | −5·9 | 36·3 | See table | |
| 11·4 | −6·0 | 37·6 | ← | |
| 11·8 | −6·1 | 38·9 | ft. | |
| 12·2 | −6·2 | 40·1 | 70 — 8·1 | |
| 12·6 | −6·3 | 41·5 | 75 — 8·4 | |
| 13·0 | −6·4 | 42·8 | 80 — 8·7 | |
| 13·4 | −6·5 | 44·2 | 85 — 8·9 | |
| 13·8 | −6·6 | 45·5 | 90 — 9·2 | |
| 14·2 | −6·7 | 46·9 | 95 — 9·5 | |
| 14·7 | −6·8 | 48·4 | | |
| 15·1 | −6·9 | 49·8 | 100 — 9·7 | |
| 15·5 | −7·0 | 51·3 | 105 — 9·9 | |
| 16·0 | −7·1 | 52·8 | 110 — 10·2 | |
| 16·5 | −7·2 | 54·3 | 115 — 10·4 | |
| 16·9 | −7·3 | 55·8 | 120 — 10·6 | |
| 17·4 | −7·4 | 57·4 | 125 — 10·8 | |
| 17·9 | −7·5 | 58·9 | | |
| 18·4 | −7·6 | 60·5 | | |
| 18·8 | −7·7 | 62·1 | 130 — 11·1 | |
| 19·3 | −7·8 | 63·8 | 135 — 11·3 | |
| 19·8 | −7·9 | 65·4 | 140 — 11·5 | |
| 20·4 | −8·0 | 67·1 | 145 — 11·7 | |
| 20·9 | −8·1 | 68·8 | 150 — 11·9 | |
| 21·4 | | 70·5 | 155 — 12·1 | |

The corrected sextant angle, in degrees and minutes, and the difference in feet between the height of the object and the observer's height of eye, are entered into Bowditch (Vol. II, 1975), Table 9, *Distance by Vertical Angle,* and the distance-off is read out directly. If the base of the observed object is within the distance to your visible horizon, Bowditch, Table 22—the instructions for its use are contained in the same volume—is entered in place of the regular Dip table.

For the small-boat navigator without Table 9, but with a hand-held, slide-rule type calculator or the equivalent aboard, a short-cut solution when relatively close to an object can be found by multiplying the charted height in feet by 0.00016 and dividing that product by the tangent of the sextant angle corrected only for index error. The answer will be the distance-off in nautical miles, and it works out reasonably well for angles greater that 0° 20', and distances within four miles.

Horizontal sextant angles are of a very high order of accuracy and can be used when position-fixing with precision is required. The line of position is obtained independently of compass direction, it being necessary only to measure the angular *difference* between the bearings to two objects. In this procedure, the sextant is held horizontally, mirror side up, and the left-most of a pair of charted objects viewed as the horizon while the right-hand object is brought to it.

Figure 6-5 illustrates one graphic method of deriving a single line of position from a pair of charted objects and can be performed right on the chart. In this example, the horizontal angle between objects *A* and *B,* as measured by sextant, is 73°. First, a line is drawn on the chart in any convenient direction toward your approximate position from either of the objects. Next, with your protractor, locate mythical point *P,* where the angle between the line you have drawn and a line to the second object is exactly 73°.

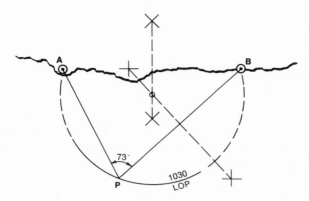

*Figure 6–5. Obtaining a line of position from a Horizontal Angle—Point P is found by plotting the observed angle between the bearings to A and B. The center of a circle is determined from the intersection of the perpendicular bisectors of sides AB and BP. The arc line of position is the circumference of the circle with radius from center to any of the three points.*

The third step is to locate the center of the circle passing through the two charted objects and point *P*, which is done by constructing the perpendicular bisectors of any two sides of the triangle formed by *A, B* and *P*. A perpendicular bisector, in case you had forgotten, is constructed by setting a pair of compasses to any length greater than the distance between the two selected points and scribing arcs on each side of the connecting line from each of the points. The line joining the two pairs of intersecting arcs is the perpendicular bisector. In Figure 6-5, we arbitrarily selected the sides *AB* and *BP* to bisect, but any two pairs would do.

From the intersection of the bisectors, which is the center of the circle, that part of the circumference we will use as our "line" of position is drawn with the radius equal to the distance to any of the three points, *A,*

*B* or *P.* As you are already aware, the resulting line of position can be combined with any others to produce a fix.

Carrying this technique a step further, if a third, charted object can be identified, and the horizontal angles between the center one and each of the other two measured at the same time, a simultaneous fix, called a "three-point fix," can be obtained. In the example in Figure 6-6, the angle measured at 1030 between objects *A* and *C* is 51°, and between *A* and *B*, 28°. Two lines of position have been derived from that information and their intersection is the 1030 Fix. Notice that the fix has been obtained without regard to the compass direction, the special feature of this technique. Had the compass bearings of each of the three objects been available to the navigator, alternatively he could have plotted those three bearings which would have intersected at the same point.

*Figure 6–6. The intersection of two lines of position from the two Horizontal Angles, AB and AC, produces a three-point fix.*

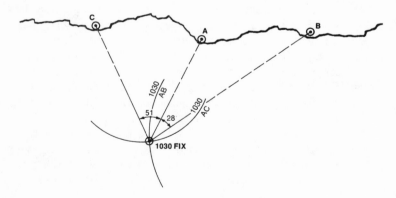

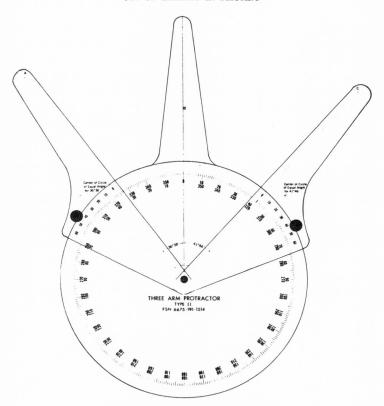

FIGURE 1102b.—Use of three-arm protractor.

*Figure 6–7. A Three-Arm Protractor—The right angle is set for 41° 46', the left angle for 36° 38'.*

A fast and easy way to obtain a three-point fix is by a device known as a three-arm protractor, or "station pointer," a model of which is shown in Figure 6-7. The left and right, movable arms are set to the respective sextant angles, left and right of the fixed, center arm. Then, by trial and error, the protractor is moved about on the chart so that the hairlines on the three arms pass through the three objects. At that position, the fix is located at the center hole of the protractor. In selecting objects for three-point fixes, the best results are obtained when the angles are of the order of 30°, or more, and the nearer they are equal, the better. The only situation to look out for is that in which all three objects *and* the observer are on or near the circumference of the same circle. That case is called the "revolver" and the fix becomes indeterminate. It is easy enough to avoid, however, by just making sure that the center object is nearest the observer. Sextant angles are not used on small boats to the extent that compass bearings are but, if you have a sextant aboard and seek high-precision position-fixing such as required by hydrographic surveyors or predicted loggers, the technique is useful to know.

Regardless of how you derive your fix, it is probably a better position than your DR and so it is common practice to start your DR plot anew from the fix and carry it forward until the next fix. An estimate of the "current" affecting your track can also be made at the time of a fix by comparing the DR position with the fix. The direction of the offset is the *set* of the current, while the distance divided by the elapsed time is the *drift*.

As a review of the piloting procedures, let's continue the practical exercise started in Figure 5-2, which is repeated and carried forward in Figure 6-8. Following a series of courses and speeds, we had tracked the vessel from its noon departure to the 1228 DR position in the vicinity of Gong Buoy "24A." At this point the navigator found that he had the buoy and the tripod on Copps

*Figure 6–8. Piloting—A continuing plot of a Dead Reckoning Track confirmed or corrected by frequent fixes from Departure at 1200 to Arrival at Entrance Channel at 1259.*

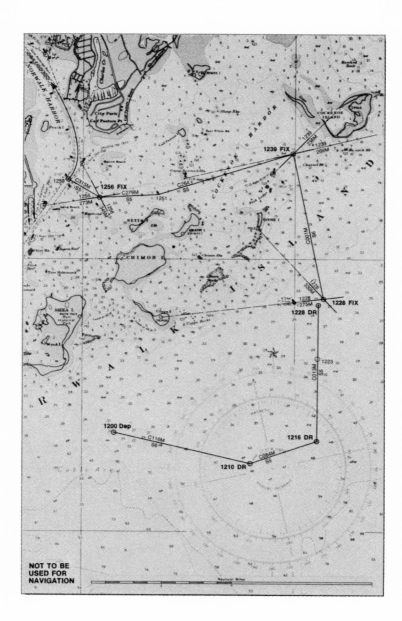

NOT TO BE
USED FOR
NAVIGATION

Island in range and, at the same time, the pole on the south end of Goose Island bore 330° Magnetic. Plotting these two lines of position, he established his 1228 Fix and restarted the DR plot from there. Although he noticed that the current had offset his track slightly in the earlier legs, the navigator found in consulting his current table that the time of slack water before the next flood began was near and, so, he elected not to compensate in setting his new course for the East entrance of Cockenoe Harbor.

After changing course to 001° M, the vessel's speed was increased to six knots and the DR track projected to the next turning point which the navigator estimated to reach at 1239. As he proceeded on course he observed, just before his ETA (Estimated Time of Arrival), that he passed about midway between the bell and nun buoys at the channel entrance, thereby confirming that the vessel was approximately on track. The depth finder which, you will recall, had been used at 1223 to pinpoint the time of crossing the five-fathom curve, was kept running as a further check against straying off course and into shoal water.

At 1239, a bearing was taken on Peck Ledge Light, reading 236° M, and next on Grassy Hammock Rocks Beacon, at 269° M. The navigator correctly observed Peck Ledge first as its bearing was changing more rapidly. The 1239 Fix coincided with the DR, indicating that the estimate of course, speed and current had been correct. The course was then changed to 264° M, heading for Can Buoy "9" and, respecting the channel speed limit, the speed was reduced to five knots.

A check on the track was provided when the Grassy Hammock Beacon was passed close aboard at a nine foot depth, and both course and speed were reconfirmed when Can "9" was reached at 1251, the estimated time of arrival. Shaping his course for the next turning point, the navigator instructed the helmsman to steer 279° M.

At 1256, bearings were taken on Beacons "14" and "11," in that order, and the lines of position plotted to produce the 1256 Fix. From that point, the course was altered to 315° M, heading directly for Can Buoy "13" on the west side of the Norwalk Entrance Channel. Arriving in mid-channel at 1259, the navigator turned northeast and, leaving the red marks to starboard and the black to port, followed the improved channel to a point opposite Can "19" from where he entered the South Anchorage Basin to anchor.

There are several points to note particularly in this exercise. While floating navaids were observed, and in two cases used as turning marks, the fixes depended upon stationary objects so that the position was reliable even had a buoy been off-station. In clear weather, with a shallow-draft vessel, it might not have been necessary to follow the track with such precision nor to take as many fixes. But if we assume that our navigator's vessel draws seven feet, and the visibility was reduced by patchy fog, you will readily agree that the detail and precision were essential. This is the important area of *judgment* which contributes so much to the successful practice of navigation.

At times, as might be the case in sailing along a relatively featureless coast, you may be able to identify only a single object suitable for observation and can, as a consequence, get only one line of position. What then? You can't derive a conventional fix from just a single line but it can still be used in a number of constructive ways. One of these is by taking a simultaneous reading of the depth finder. You will recall in our piloting exercise, Figure 6–8, that the navigator checked the time he crossed the five-fathom curve, 1223, as a confirmation of his speed along his track. Again, in the vicinity of Grassy Hammock Beacon, the depth reading backed up his rough positional check. Quite often, and especially if the bottom contours are irregular, it is possible to plot a single line of position and estimate from a depth sounding (corrected for the state of the tide when necessary) the probable point on the position line at which you are located.

In a like manner, though the opportunities are far less frequent, a line of position (in the form of an arc) obtained from a distance-off measurement can be scribed on the chart and the probable location on that line pinpointed by matching the measured depth with the charted soundings.

Still another way of obtaining an approximate line to cross with a single, observed line of position is to take a series of soundings at fixed intervals and plot them on a strip of paper at the same scale as the chart. Then the strip is "fitted" to an area along and parallel to your course line on the chart where a similar series of soundings coincides. A variation of this, which works satisfactorily when the bottom contours are sufficiently regular, is to sail along a constant depth curve, maintaining the depth by maneuvering the vessel. Then, the intersection of a single visual bearing with that depth curve on the chart indicates your probable position.

A position line by itself, if at right angles to your course, can tell you whether your speed over the bottom is running ahead or behind your reckoned position. A line ahead or astern can tell you whether you are to the right or left of your intended course. Ranges, formed by two marks in line, make ideal leading marks for this purpose.

While not of the quality of a conventional fix, Estimated Positions derived from single lines of position and any other reliable information which can be applied are almost always better than a dead reckoning position alone. Although it is not common practice to replot the DR track from such a position, it is important to take cognizance of the EP so that your projected courses between fixes do not lead into danger.

Sometimes it is not as important to know where you are as it is to know where you are *not.* This involves the practice of using a single line as a danger bearing or danger angle. As an example, in Figure 6-9 there is a submerged, unmarked reef rising steeply from the bottom so that soundings alone will not give sufficient warning when approaching it. The reef is between you and a point marked with a high tower, about 0.8 miles from the point and practically on your course. A danger bearing is plotted from the point, just clearing the reef, and is measured to be 357°. Your *observed* bearing of the point is, presently, 002°, but you are not certain as to exactly how far along the track you are. You can see that

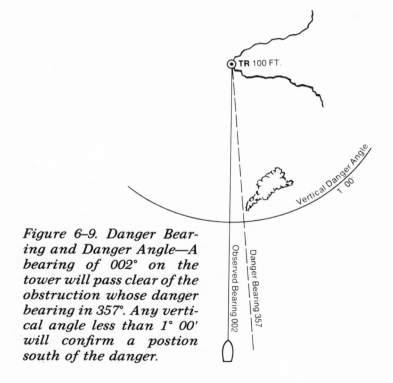

*Figure 6–9. Danger Bearing and Danger Angle—A bearing of 002° on the tower will pass clear of the obstruction whose danger bearing in 357°. Any vertical angle less than 1° 00' will confirm a postion south of the danger.*

as long as the observed bearing remains *greater* than the danger bearing, you are in safe water. Heading for the point on course 002°, therefore, will clear the obstruction.

It is also possible, though less frequently as practicable, to precompute a vertical danger angle, in this case 1° 00'. Then, by measuring the actual vertical angle of the high tower with a sextant as you approach, you know you will be south of the reef and in deep water as long as the sextant angle reads below 1°.

A frequently used method of utilizing single lines of position is the "running fix," a position determined by crossing lines of position taken at different times and advanced (or "retired") to a common time. Figure 6-10 illustrates the principle and technique. On course 290° at five knots, the navigator plots a line of position from Beacon *A* which bears 028° at eleven o'clock. One hour later, the bearing on *A* is taken again and is 075°. The 1100 line is then advanced the distance traveled along the course—in this case, 5 miles in the hour elapsed— and the advanced line drawn parallel to the first at the point of advance. The intersection of the plotted 1200 line, and the 1100 line advanced to 1200, is the 1200 Running Fix.

Restarting the plot, the navigator next gets a single bearing of Beacon *B,* bearing 357° at 1330. This position line is crossed with the 1200 bearing on *A* which is advanced 7.5 miles along the course line—the distance traveled in the elapsed time—producing a running fix from bearings of two objects taken at different times, just as the running fix was produced by two bearings of the same object taken at different times in the first instance.

Position lines obtained by any other means can also be combined in a running fix plot. Do notice the form of labeling the lines to avoid confusion, the advanced (or retired) lines always being identified with the time they

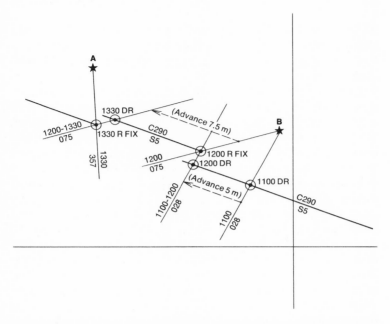

*Figure 6-10. The Running Fix—The 1200 R Fix is produced by the intersection of the 1200 bearing on A and the 1100 bearing on A advanced to 1200. The 1330 R Fix is produced by the intersection of the 1330 bearing on B and the 1200 bearing on A advanced to 1330.*

were taken followed by the time to which adjusted. As you will readily understand, a running fix is only as accurate as your estimate of the course and distance over which the line of position is transferred. As a consequence, it is normal practice to use as short a time interval as practical, allowing for adequate "spread" (30° or more if possible) between the intersecting lines. If course or speed changes take place during the elapsed period between bearings, the position line can be moved, just like the vessel, along the plotted track. Just be sure to construct the new line at the point of use exactly parallel with the original.

There are several special cases in which the information from a running fix derived from successive bearings of a single object can be had without having to plot the fix on the chart. One such case is called "bow and beam" bearings, in which the first bearing is taken when the object is exactly 45 degrees ("broad on the bow") from the vessel's heading, and the second when it is exactly 90 degrees ("abeam"). Then, the distance run between the bearings is equal to the distance-off when abeam.

A second case is called, "doubling the angle on the bow." In this, the relative bearing from the ship's heading between the first and second observations is exactly doubled. The run between the bearings is the distance at which the vessel will be from the object at the time of the second bearing. Other such relationships can be determined and solved mathematically but, because it is quite difficult to make all the precise measurements on a small boat and, especially since by plotting on the chart the navigator can better visualize his position in relation to his surroundings, the graphic method for running fixes—which can be done at the navigator's time and convenience—is almost universally preferred.

Lines, lines, lines. Course lines, position lines, range lines, danger bearing lines; all are the navigator's implements for the safe positioning of his vessel. Learn to think in these terms and you'll be well on your way to qualifying as a practical navigator.

# 7. Navigation at Night and in Fog

Navigation at night imposes additional demands on the navigator's skill. The relationship of near and distant geographical features on which you rely, consciously or unconsciously, during the day cannot be discerned—except, to a degree, by radar. Instead, reliance must be placed on lighted navigational aids and careful piloting. In coastwise navigation at night it is particularly important to follow definite courses from point to point and to maintain a meticulous plot so you have a good estimate of your position at all times.

Fortunately, most of the coastal areas visited by yachtsmen are well provided with lighted navaids. The light characteristics of major installations, such as lighthouses, are indicated on the chart and detailed in the *Light List*. Distinctive combinations are used on lights in close proximity to avoid confusion. The distance at which principal lights can be seen under normal conditions is also shown, to the nearest mile, in the charts and publications. That range is either the maximum distance at which the earth's curvature permits seeing the light from a height of fifteen feet or, if the light is of low intensity, the maximum distance it can be seen in clear weather. Since the height of eye on a yacht is often less than fifteen feet, the actual range may be a mile or so less than indicated. There are other circumstances too, like haze or abnormal atmospheric conditions, background loom from city lights and so forth, which make the determination of *exact* range problematical. The range of visibility, therefore, should always be dealt with as an approximation.

It is a good idea, if you are making for a light some distance away, to draw an arc on your chart at the probable visible range and estimate the time of arrival at the intersection of the arc with your course. If the night is clear and the light of proper intensity, it should appear on the horizon close to the appointed time. Sometimes, if you are waiting nervously for it to appear, the light or its loom may be spotted a little earlier by elevating your vantage point. If there is a sea running when you first pick up a light on the horizon, watch it for a moment before you make a positive identification. A "flashing" light may turn out to be the fixed light of another vessel disappearing and reappearing with the swells. When the characteristic is clearly identifiable, your stopwatch may be useful if you can't estimate the time sequence with sufficient accuracy by yourself.

Channel markers, including all the lighted, floating navaids, display light characteristics consistent with their color, shape and placement as part of the lateral system of buoyage. The extract of Chart No. 1 in the Appendix illustrates the various combinations and how they are used. All these aids are included in the *Light List* and identified on the chart by a symbol and a brief legend.

A special class of inshore navigational aid, particularly useful at night, is the lighted range. Usually located at harbor entrances or to mark the centerline of a channel, ranges are formed in pairs with the rear light higher than the front one. Normally, the range lights are displayed from the same structures used for ranges in the daytime and they may exhibit highly directional beams, or special colors or characteristics, to avoid confusion with lighted aids nearby.

In a congested area, it is not uncommon to see a number of flashing lights at the same time. It can be quite confusing, especially against the backdrop of a brightly lighted area ashore. Here again is where a careful plot and a reliable compass come to your rescue. If you know where you are, and you have a good bearing on the light, chances are the identification of it will be quick and easy. Otherwise it may be necessary to approach the mark closely enough for visual identification—not always a safe practice in restricted waters.

You should remind yourself frequently of the dictum mentioned earlier, to avoid total reliance on lights, especially in minor navaids. Most of the major installations have back-up systems to take over if the main light fails, but the smaller buoys do not. While the record of dependability is remarkable, lights do, on occasion, exhibit faulty characteristics or go out altogether. If you are confident of your plot you will probably find the buoy anyway or, if it is equipped with a sound device, hear it before you arrive. As with many of the unlighted aids you encounter in inshore waters, most lighted buoys are also marked with reflective material to facilitate spotting and identifying by searchlight. A pair of binoculars, like the standard Navy 7 × 50's with good light-gathering power, makes the job easier but there is still no substitute for precision piloting when finding your way home through hazardous waters in darkness.

Electronic aids may also offer a major assist at night. Away from shore, the coastal radiobeacons can provide lines of position from which an approximate fix can be derived, while inshore, the low-powered beacons, often placed strategically at harbor entrances, may be "homed" on (by orienting the antenna dead ahead and altering the vessel's course until the null is found) to a point where the lighted aids take over.

Loran yields lines of position, usually more precise than those obtained by RDF, from whence the navigator can proceed by dead reckoning until inshore navaids are identified. Radar is, of course, the most valuable electronic tool for this purpose. Not only can it spot navigational aids and distinctive geographical features, but it can also produce range and bearing information for position fixing. Radar really comes into its own, however, in its primary application, collision avoidance at night or in periods of reduced visibility.

It takes practice to spot, identify and determine the orientation and relative movement of other ships at sea. The navigator needs to be familiar with the lights required on various classes of vessels (referring, if necessary, to the 72 COLREGS and Rules for Inland Waters published in the *Navigation Rules,* CG-169, described in Chapter 1). It is always a good procedure on seeing the lights of an approaching vessel to start taking a series of bearings to ascertain whether it will pass ahead, is opening with your course or, if the bearing remains steady, is on a collision course with you. It is still better practice, if the other ship is a big one, to keep out of the way entirely—it is required by law in confined waters. A large ship simply may not be able to see you, much less avoid you when she does. A cardinal rule for a small-boat navigator is *never* to pass ahead of a larger, powered vessel unless you are absolutely certain of *your* relative position and *his* intentions.

The navigator's relatively comfortable world changes completely when fog shuts in. Gone is any visual reference to the shore and, in thick fog, only those objects which can be approached within a few yards may ever be seen. Geographical orientation becomes difficult, if not downright confusing, and dependence on your instruments is the order of the day. Precise information on your vessel's position and movement is vital and the maintenance of a perfect plot is more important than ever. In essence, if you have not yet developed confidence through experience in your instruments and your piloting ability, you are well advised to postpone venturing forth in a fog until you have that confidence as it will be an unnerving experience if not a hazardous one.

But navigators do venture forth, and with safety, when the fundamentals have been mastered. Fog is not a condition to be feared, but it does command the utmost respect from the entire ship's company and the total attention of the navigator. That attention rightfully starts *before* fog is encountered by checking and rechecking the compass, the depth finder, the speed or distance measuring instruments, as well as any other electronic equipment aboard, during periods of good visibility. In this way you are prepared when called upon and, with the careful plot you should have been running habitually, you will have a point of departure should fog close in suddenly.

Approaching a landfall, the navigator may be able to utilize RDF bearings or Loran lines for positioning or, by maneuvering into a position while still in deep water which would place a floating navaid, preferably audible, between him and a radiobeacon, "home" on the radio signal until the buoy is intercepted. Except for radar, which is probably the best device to have aboard under these circumstances, the depth finder or lowly lead line may be your best indication of approach to danger if the bottom contour is at all cooperative.

From a known position, the navigator in fog usually sets his course in legs as short as possible, often hopping from buoy to buoy even if it extends his total distance. The course and the speed, which should be moderated in fog to the extent that you can stop or maneuver within your range of visibility, must be monitored precisely and each mark positively identified before proceeding to the next. A good procedure, called "running your time," is to precalculate your estimated time of arrival at each mark from the previous one, figuring your projected speed by applying your best estimate of the effect of the current. By timing with a watch you determine when you have "run your time" and stop, look and listen, or circle slowly until you see or hear the aid you are seeking. If you miss finding a mark promptly in hazardous waters or, if you become otherwise unsure of your position, the only sensible alternatives are to consider anchoring or turning offshore until conditions improve. Most beginners seem to be reluctant to do this, presumably because the sanctuary of a cozy, shoreside berth appears irresistible, but the seasoned navigator does not hesitate to choose one of the safer, though temporarily less comfortable, alternatives. I've never met a good navigator who, in retrospect, regretted his choice.

Aside from electronic instrumentation and your plot, audible navigational aids are your source of positioning information in fog. The characteristics of major fog signals are given in the *Light List* and your stopwatch may be called into play to make a positive identification. The type of audible device installed on the lesser aids is indicated on the chart. Caution should be exercised in relying on floating aids since those devices depending on wave action may not sound at all in calm water. Upwind, sounds are notoriously hard to hear and to pinpoint in bearing. Sometimes it is safe to approach a bold shore and, if it can be done from the lee side, the fog will frequently "scale up" just enough to provide a momentary glimpse.

The navigator in fog has to be alert to everything—bells, whistles, motor noises, the cry of gulls on a ledge, the sound of breaking waves; yes, even barking dogs ashore—which might contribute to his estimate of his position. Current flow around buoys or other anchored objects is particularly noted since, at the moderated speed, the effect of any current will be more pronounced than it is at normal cruising speeds. The depth finder, if available, is kept going continuously and the observation of the changing bottom contours also added to the navigator's store of information.

The wear and tear on the nerves notwithstanding, probably the most serious danger in fog, and especially in crowded, commercial waterways, is the danger of collision with another vessel. Having your radar reflector in place is of help and with radar itself aboard you can probably proceed with safety. Otherwise, the best advice, if you have a choice, may be to avoid the confrontation altogether until conditions improve. After all, you wouldn't cross Times Square blindfolded for pleasure.

The fog signals you should make, as well as those required of other types of vessels, are also part of the 72 COLREGS and Rules for Inland Waters found in *Navigation Rules,* CG-169. Large, commercial vessels are usually meticulous in sounding their required fog signals. Many smaller vessels and yachts, unfortunately, are not. As a consequence, you must never relax your guard in fog. Stay alert, listen carefully and be safe.

# 8. Safe Anchoring

The technique of anchoring is usually considered to be one of the rudiments of seamanship but, in the practice of *safe* anchoring, the navigator can and does play an important part in the "when, where and how" of the process.

"When to anchor?" is a question normally answered by "When the skipper decides to," and implies a snug anchorage at the conclusion of a passage or at the end of an exhilerating day's sail. But the navigator may need to suggest other times, too. Should you, for example, have calculated from the *Tidal Current Tables* (described in Chapter 1) that you are going to arrive in a low-powered vessel at a place like Hell Gate just before the predicted time of maximum adverse current, you might be well advised to anchor and await favorable conditions—the common practice in the old, sailing-ship days. Similarly, should the navigator estimate his time of arrival in the vicinity of a bridge with limited opening hours or one with restricted overhead clearance so that he could pass only at low water, temporary anchoring may be the safest and most practical tactic.

One of the most difficult admissions for any navigator to make is that he is lost, or at least disoriented and unsure of his position. When this occurs at night, or particularly in fog, anchoring should always be considered as a primary alternative to forging ahead. Under the tension of picking your way through hazardous waters and the discomforts brought on by darkness and fatigue, not to mention the dungeon-like aspect of a thick fog, the human tendency is to press on to the illusory comfort of your intended destination. But it may be far, far safer to drop the hook where you are and wait for conditions when you can sort things out. Needless to say, this is most practical, and desirable, when you are in relatively shallow water as is usually the case in the vicinity of dangers in coastal waters. Offshore, of course, or anywhere with adequate sea room, you might elect to stand away from dangers as a practical alternative. The ancient seaman's adage, "when in doubt, anchor," finds numerous chances for application in the modern yacht which cruises adventurously.

Selecting the place to anchor is another exercise in which the small-boat navigator can make a contribution to the safety of the vessel and the comfort of her crew. If protection from wind and wave or a strong current is sought, and particularly if a storm is predicted, the navigator may be the first source of advice as to the quality of an anchorage from the point of view of the protection afforded by the adjacent land and the nature of the holding ground from the charted bottom characteristics. Publications like the *Coast Pilot* (Chapter 1) may also provide the navigator with information on the location of harbors of refuge or of Special Anchorage areas within a harbor complex suitable for small craft.

Having chosen the area in which the vessel intends to anchor, the navigator has also to consider the route of safe approach, often paramount under conditions of reduced visibility. If he has chosen a particularly secluded spot, it may call for the most precise piloting of the day and an up-to-date knowledge of the state of the tide and current to arrive without grounding.

Inside an anchorage, the navigator can help pick a spot in relation to other anchored vessels through his knowledge of the rise and fall of the tide expected and the anticipated strength and direction of wind and current.

Commonly in naval and larger commercial vessels, though only occasionally in yachts, a berth is selected or assigned at a fixed position within an anchorage area. The particular berth is then located by the navigator by taking bearings of nearby objects on his chart. For example, had the navigator been assigned an anchorage berth at the location of the 0905 Fix in Figure 6-2, he would have located it by the bearings of the objects ashore or, lacking compass bearings, by the ranges which conveniently existed. In approaching his berth, the common practice is to run in on one range as a leading mark and drop the anchor when the other range (or compass bearing) comes to its proper reading.

After anchoring, either in a prescribed berth or one of his own choosing, the navigator wants to make certain he is safely anchored and not dragging. This can be done by taking and recording bearings of fixed objects which can be rechecked periodically, or, if in a designated berth, by bearings on the same objects or ranges used for the approach. A convenient check for a yacht which has anchored independently or has picked up a strange mooring is to identify one or two natural ranges ashore, such as a tree in line with the window of a house which, by remaining steady, provide confirmation that you are at the spot in which you anchored. The process is just a simple adaptation of the principles of position finding but under the easier conditions of a stationary vessel.

How to anchor, as we have agreed, is primarily an exercise in seamanship but, here again, the navigator can provide a strong assist. By knowing the state of the tide and its anticipated range from the *Tide Tables,* the effect on "scope" can be estimated. If, for example, a yacht anchors in six feet of water and chooses a safe 7-to-1 ratio for the scope of the anchor rode, that 42-foot length becomes only a very marginal 3-to-1 ratio if the tide rises eight feet. By the same token on a falling tide, as the depth of the water decreases with a constant length of rode out, the yacht requires an increasing amount of swinging room. The navigator has to take this into account in selecting a berth in a crowded anchorage. Incidentally, in using a depth finder to check depths in an anchorage which may be critical for your vessel, remember that the transducer may be located *several feet* below your waterline and the readings have to be corrected to get the precise depth.

The type of "set" can be another decision in which the navigator's information may be invaluable. In questionable holding ground, he might want to suggest another type of anchor if available ("lightweight" anchors which are so superb in mud are notoriously poor in kelp, for example). If anchored in a tideway with a strong and complete reversal of the current expected, it is often good judgment to set two anchors, one with, and one against the current, so that when the current does reverse, the load will be taken on the up-stream anchor and the other will not break out and have to reset itself. If an anchorage is to be alongside a channel, and the area outside the channel shoals rapidly, the only location available may be parallel to, and just outside the channel where a fore-and-aft, two-anchor set may be called for to avoid the danger of swinging into a trafficked fairway.

Should a storm be anticipated, it is sound practice while lying to one anchor set for the prevailing condition, to set another in the direction from which storm winds or seas are expected to come. Then, as in a tideway, the danger of breaking out the first hook and dragging it under storm conditions until it resets itself is considerably lessened. Obviously such storm conditions also call for the heaviest ground tackle and rodes you have on board.

In today's typically crowded anchorages, the swinging room available in your selected berth may simply preclude the use of sufficient scope to provide a margin of safety at high water. Here again, a two-anchor set may recommend itself not only to reduce the swinging room, and the amount of "skating" about which is characteristic of a yacht, but also to provide that good night's sleep the extra security of a second hook offers.

A yacht may actually spend as much of her life at anchor as she does underway. Safe anchoring, therefore, may be as important to the security of the vessel as is safe navigation.

# 9. Practical Wrinkles

Experience, as we agreed at the outset, is the ingredient necessary to temper the science of navigation with those elements which are still in the realm of art. But there is no reason why some of the devices of the practical navigator shouldn't be yours to borrow and to apply to your own knowledge as you progress.

Perhaps the most understated of all the strategems of the experienced navigator is his concern with planning and preparation—"forehandedness" we called it in the Introduction. Checking to see that all the charts and publications for the voyage are aboard and up-to-date, is an obvious first step. Plotting courses and figuring distances, noting the times of tides and currents, in short, many of the things a pilot does in filing a flight plan, can all be done before leaving the berth and under more comfortable circumstances, as you're likely to discover, than after you're underway and everything is happening at once.

Always a good idea on your own boat, but especially

if you assume the navigator's duties on another, is to test the navigation equipment before you depart. Many an unpleasant surprise can be avoided when conditions at sea deteriorate suddenly, *if* the navigator knows beforehand the operation and reliability of the equipment he is counting on to get him home safely.

The well prepared navigator is also ever alert, since the *art* of navigation certainly includes running observation of the surrounding scene. Noticing the current flow at buoys, the direction of smoke rising ashore, the build-up of clouds overhead—all the sights and sounds which add to the navigator's store of information—together bear on the effectiveness of his navigation. The so-called "Seaman's Eye" is really just that, and the ability to notice, estimate and judge from the phenomena around you is the reward for constant and thoughtful observation.

There is a legitimate process called "eyeball navigation" that is akin to the "Seaman's Eye." This involves the utilization of such things as the color of the water, which in the tropics can give a good indication of depth, objects selected to provide ranges or leading marks, and other "free" assists to the observant practitioner. Approaching Palm Beach at night, for example, with an unknown set from the Gulf Stream, the approximate location of the narrow entrance channel can be picked out from among the myriad lights of the city while well offshore simply by "eyeballing" the brilliant lights of landing aircraft at the nearby airport. Off the coast of Maine and in the Great Lakes, ferries and Lake steamers follow prescribed tracks. "Eyeballing" their movements can give you helpful navigational information. Entering a strange port you may also gather "free" and safe sailing directions by watching the movements of a large vessel whose draft relegates it to the main fairways and to waters several times your required depth.

Underway, the practical navigator takes advantage of

every opportunity to check on his dead reckoning. Look back, as well as ahead, to detect drift from your intended track. Use your depth finder constantly to confirm your position estimate or to warn of impending danger. Check off the buoys as you pass them so you don't get confused in a busy waterway, and note on the chart for your return voyage any changes in the buoyage you discover. Where practical, plan your course to intercept buoys along your track, especially in low visibility, so you have a "free" position check before approaching a hazardous area. A modicum of common sense and an observant navigator can do a great deal to keep a vessel located and safe even without the more formal procedures.

A chart is a bird's-eye view of the area through which you are sailing. Learning to project one's self into the surface view from any point on the chart is an undertaking requiring a little practice but is well worth the effort. A corollary to this is to confirm the reasonableness of the courses and positions you have plotted by actually going out to take a look after you have done your chart work, to see if your situation isn't exactly as it should appear to an observer at the chart's surface. Here again, there is simply no substitute for a thinking, reasoning and observing navigator.

We have talked a lot about currents and how experienced navigators "play" them to make the best use of time and fuel on a passage. As we saw in Chapter 5, the difference in speed made good that can be gained by proper planning and timing is well worth the effort spent. If drift from your track—the "leeway" common to sailing vessels on the wind—is your concern, an observation of the angle between your wake and your heading may give a good indication. Sailing through a current, if you haven't determined the course to steer by pre-calculation, you can often find a range on the shore to use as a leading mark and stay on that range by adjusting your heading. Where the current tables don't give you the direction of flow or predicted times for your particular location, it may be possible from the times of high and low water at nearby points to make an adequate approximation. If you think of the coastline and its adjacent waters as the edge of a large basin which fills and drains, a little imagination may give you an idea of the probable direction, and even the strength, of the current flow.

You can use knowledge of the state of the tide to good advantage, too. A good idea in entering an area in which the charted depths appear at all critical is to plan your approach for half-tide while it is rising. At that time you probably have a comfortable margin over the chart sounding datum even if minor shoaling has taken place since the chart was published. Above all, if you should ground, the rising tide will enable you to float off with little more than an embarrassed expression. Approaching a bridge or overhead obstruction with critical clearance, the time of low water and the direction of current flow, if known in advance, can also save you considerable time and anxiety.

A category of onboard equipment we have only touched upon is the rapidly evolving field of hand-held, electronic calculators. Most of the exercises in coastwise navigation have been worked out, traditionally, by graphic methods, even though a mathematical solution is possible, because of the time required and the opportunity for error in a long, tedious computation. With the modern calculator, however, all this changes and a tedious mathematical calculation becomes a practicality.

Time-speed-distance problems and the like require only basic arithmetic and the simplest type of calculator which performs just the four arithmetic functions will suffice. Current sailing and distance-off problems are examples using plane trigonometry and require the next level of "scientific" calculator—one having trig functions and polar/rectangular convertibility for vector arithmetic. You have still another choice, between manually operated calculators where you make every key punch, and the "programmed" types (programmed either by you or the manufacturer) in which you enter the initial data and the "program" steps through a pre-arranged key-punch sequence to the solution. Some of the equipment is quite sophisticated (and quite expensive). Your choice has to be made on the basis of the kinds of problems you are to solve and what the convenience is worth to you.

Underlying every calculator solution is the fact that the instrument is only a processing device and can neither think for you nor expand your knowledge. This means that the navigator should be thoroughly grounded in the principles of the science and call on the calculator as a means of facilitating the computation rather than a short-cut way to learn the science. It must also be recognized that the environment on a small boat at sea is notoriously inhospitable to delicate electronic equipment and the supply of energy for powering or recharging may not always be unlimited. The prudent navigator who chooses the convenience of a calculator should, therefore, provide himself with alternate means of solution against the day when the inevitable malfunction appears. For navigators who are mathematically inclined, working out solutions and programming them on a calculator is an entertaining pastime. Most of the formulae you need can be found in Bowditch, *American Practical Navigator,* Vol. I, Appendix T, or *The Yachtsman's Guide to Calculator Navigation.*

At the risk of sounding contradictory, I would like to add the suggestion that the accomplished navigator resist the temptation to "over-navigate." By this I mean engaging the entire ship's company in the act and making a large-scale production out of the simplest procedure. The game is not to impress your crew with your own navigational acumen nor to over-dramatize the actual practice, for your fellow crew members can become bored, if not downright annoyed, and may not take you seriously when the time comes.

Throughout this book we have described the discipline of navigation and have emphasized the elements necessary to perform it safely and with common sense. But one should not overlook the crowning personal enjoyment, pride, and satisfaction which comes from a job well done—a passage at sea made safely and according to plan.

# Glossary

*Bearing*—The horizontal direction of a line between two points on the surface of the earth.

*Binnacle*—The base or stand in which a compass is housed.

*Characteristic*—The identifying color and period of a light; the identifying signal of a sound device or radio-beacon.

*Chart Sounding Datum*—The state or level of the tide to which all charted soundings are referenced.

*Course*—The direction of travel, also called the track, usually stated as a compass direction. The *course made good* is the bearing of the destination from the departure point.

*Critical Table*—A table in which a single value is tabulated for limiting increments of entry values as, for example, the *Almanac's* Dip Table.

*Current*—The sum of the elements diverting a vessel from its intended track; the hypothetical set and drift accounting for the difference between the dead reckoning position and a simultaneous fix.

*Danger Angle*—The bearing as observed from a vessel limiting the safe approach to an off-lying danger.

*Dead Reckoning* (DR)—The process of establishing a position by applying courses and distances sailed from the last known position.

*Departure*—The point or position from which a voyage, and the dead reckoning plot, commences.

*Deviation*—The difference between the magnetic direction and the compass reading; a function of the vessel's magnetic field.

*Dip* (D)—The angle between the true horizontal and the observer's line of sight to the visible horizon.

*Drift*—The rate of flow of a current.

*Estimated Position* (EP)—The most probable position of a vessel, short of a fix, determined by applying current data or other anomalies to the position determined by dead reckoning.

*Estimated Time of Arrival* (ETA)—The time determined by projecting the speed of advance of a vessel to its arrival at a designated destination.

*Fix*—A position, determined without reference to a previous position, usually resulting from the intersection of two or more lines of position. A *Running Fix* is a position derived from lines of position taken at different times and advanced (or retired) to a common time.

*Inspection Tables*—A volume of tabulated solutions from which an answer can be extracted by simple inspection.

*Interpolation*—The process of determining intermediate values between given, tabular values.

*Latitude*—The angular distance north or south of the equator.

*Leading Light*—A light so located that vessels may steer directly for it until close aboard (when a new course is taken). Also called a *Leading Mark.*

*Longitude*—The angular distance east or west of the prime meridian, (0°) located at Greenwich, England.

*Loran*—A radio-navigation system operating on the principle that the difference in the time of arrival of radio pulses from two precisely synchronized transmitting stations describes a hyperbolic line of position.

*Line of Position*—"A line on some point of which a vessel may be presumed to be located as a result of observation or measurement"—Bowditch.

*Lubber's Line*—The index, aligned with the ship's head, against which the compass card is read.

*Mercator Projection*—A projection, named after its inventor, a Flemish geographer of the sixteenth century, in which the coordinates on earth are conceived as projected on a cylinder tangent to the earth at the equator. Classified by type, it is an *equatorial cylindrical orthomorphic* projection.

*Meridian*—A great circle through the geographical poles of the earth. The meridian of Greenwich (0°) is called the *prime meridian.*

*Parallel*—A common name for a circle on earth, parallel with the equator, connecting all points of equal latitude.

*Piloting*—"Navigation involving frequent or continuous determination of position or a line of position relative to geographical points, to a high degree of accuracy"—Bowditch.

*Pilot Waters*—Waters, usually inshore, in which navigation is performed by piloting.

*Radar*—A radiolocation system in which transmission and reception take place at the same location, and which utilizes the radio-reflecting properties of objects to determine their positions.

*Range*—Two or more objects in line, or the distance of an object from an observer.

*Rhumb Line*—A line on the earth's surface which makes the same oblique angle with all the meridians.

*Set*—The direction toward which a current flows.

*Sextant Altitude* (hs)—The uncorrected angle of altitude as measured directly by sextant observation.

*Soundings*—The measured or charted depths of the water.

*Speed Made Good*—The speed actually made good, regardless of the speed through the water.

*Variation*—The difference between true and magnetic direction.

*Vector*—A straight line representing direction by its orientation, and magnitude by its length.

# Chart No. 1

## United States of America

# Nautical Chart Symbols and Abbreviations

SIXTH EDITION
JULY 1975

Prepared jointly by

**DEPARTMENT OF COMMERCE**
**National Oceanic and Atmospheric Administration**
National Ocean Survey *(Formerly Coast and Geodetic Survey, and U.S. Lake Survey)*

**DEPARTMENT OF DEFENSE**
**Defense Mapping Agency**
Hydrographic Center

Published at Washington, D.C.
**U.S. DEPARTMENT OF COMMERCE**
**National Oceanic and Atmospheric Administration**
National Ocean Survey

# GENERAL REMARKS

This publication (CHART NO. 1) contains symbols and abbreviations that have been approved for use on nautical charts published by the United States of America. The buoyage systems used by other countries often vary from that used by the United States. Charts produced by the Defense Mapping Agency Hydrographic Center (DMAHC) will show the colors, lights, and other characteristics in use for the area of the individual chart. Certain modified reproduction charts distributed by DMAHC will also show the shapes and other distinctive features that may vary from those illustrated in this chart. Terms, symbols, and abbreviations are numbered in accordance with a standard form approved by a 1952 resolution of the International Hydrographic Organization (IHO). Although the use of IHO-approved symbols and abbreviations is not mandatory, the United States has cooperated to adopt many IHO-approved symbols for standard use on U.S. nautical charts. Alphanumeric style differences in the first column of the following pages indicate symbol and abbreviation status as follows:

VERTICAL FIGURES indicate those items for which the symbol and abbreviation are in accordance with resolutions of the IHO.

SLANTING FIGURES indicate those symbols for which no IHO resolution has been adopted.

SLANTING FIGURES UNDERSCORED indicate IHO and U.S. symbols do not agree.

SLANTING FIGURES ASTERISKED indicate that no symbol has been adopted by the United States.

SLANTING FIGURES IN PARENTHESES indicate that the items are in addition to those appearing in the "Glossary of Cartographic Terms", SP No. 22, 3rd Edition, 1951, IHO, and subsequent revisions.

† All changes since the July 1972 edition of this publication are indicated by the dagger symbol in the margin immediately adjacent to the item identification of the symbol or abbreviation affected.

BUILDINGS. A conspicuous feature on a building may be shown by a landmark symbol with a descriptive label. (See I 8b, 36, 44, 72.) Prominent buildings that are of assistance to the mariner may be shown by actual shape as viewed from above (see I 3a, 19, 47, 66), and may be marked "CONSPICUOUS".

BUOYS and BEACONS. On entering a channel from seaward, buoys on starboard side are red with even numbers, on port side black with odd numbers. Lights on buoys on starboard side of channel are red or white, on port side white or green. Mid-channel buoys have black-and-white vertical stripes. Junction or obstruction buoys, which may be passed on either side, have red-and-black horizontal bands. This system does not always apply to foreign waters.

The position of a fixed beacon is represented by the center of the beacon symbol or the circle at the base of the symbol. The approximate position of a buoy is represented by the dot or circle associated with the buoy symbol. The approximate position is used because of practical limitations in positioning and maintaining buoys and their sinkers in precise geographical locations. These limitations include, but are not limited to, inherent imprecisions in position fixing methods, prevailing atmospheric and sea conditions, the slope of and the material making up the seabed, the fact that buoys are moored to sinkers by varying lengths of chain, and the fact that buoy body and/or sinker positions are not under continuous surveillance, but are normally checked only during periodic maintenance visits which often occur more than a year apart. The position of the buoy body can be expected to shift inside and outside the charting symbol due to the forces of nature. The mariner is also cautioned that buoys are liable to be carried away, shifted, capsized, sunk, etc. Lighted buoys may be extinguished or sound signals may not function as a result of ice, running ice or other natural causes, collisions, or other accidents. For the foregoing reasons, a prudent mariner must not rely completely upon the charted position or operation of floating aids to navigation, but will also utilize bearings from fixed objects and aids to navigation on shore. Further, a vessel attempting to pass close aboard always risks collision with a yawing buoy or with the obstruction the buoy marks.

COLORS are optional for characterizing various features and areas in the charts.

DEPTH contours and soundings are shown in meters on an increasing number of new charts and new editions; the depth unit is stated on all charts.

HEIGHTS of land and conspicuous objects are given in feet above Mean High Water, unless otherwise stated in the title of the chart.

IMPROVED CHANNELS are shown by limiting dashed lines with the depth and date of the latest examination placed adjacent to the channel except when the channel data is tabulated.

LETTERING styles and capitalization as indicated in Chart No. 1 are not always rigidly adhered to on the charts.

LONGITUDES are referred to the Meridian of Greenwich.

OBSOLESCENT SYMBOLIZATION on charts will be revised to agree with the current preferred usage as soon as opportunity affords.

SHORELINE shown on charts represents the line of contact between the land and a selected water elevation. In areas affected by tidal fluctuation, this line of contact is usually the mean high-water line. In confined coastal waters of diminished tidal influence, a mean water level line may be used. The shoreline of interior waters (rivers, lakes) is usually a line representing a specified elevation above a selected datum. Shoreline is symbolized by a heavy line (A 9).

APPARENT SHORELINE is used on charts to show the outer edge of marine vegetation where that limit would reasonably appear as the shoreline to the mariner or where it prevents the shoreline from being clearly defined. Apparent shoreline is symbolized by a light line (A 7, C 17).

U.S. COAST PILOTS, SAILING DIRECTIONS, LIGHT LISTS, RADIO AIDS, and related publications furnish information required by the navigator that cannot be shown conveniently on the nautical chart.

U.S. NAUTICAL CHART CATALOGS and INDEXES list nautical charts, auxiliary maps and related publications, and include general information relative to the charts.

Some differences may be observed between Chart No. 1 and symbols shown on certain reproductions of foreign charts and special charts. Foreign symbols may be interpreted by reference to the Symbol Sheet or Chart No. 1 of the originating country. A glossary of foreign terms and abbreviations is generally given on charts on which they are used, as well as in the Sailing Directions.

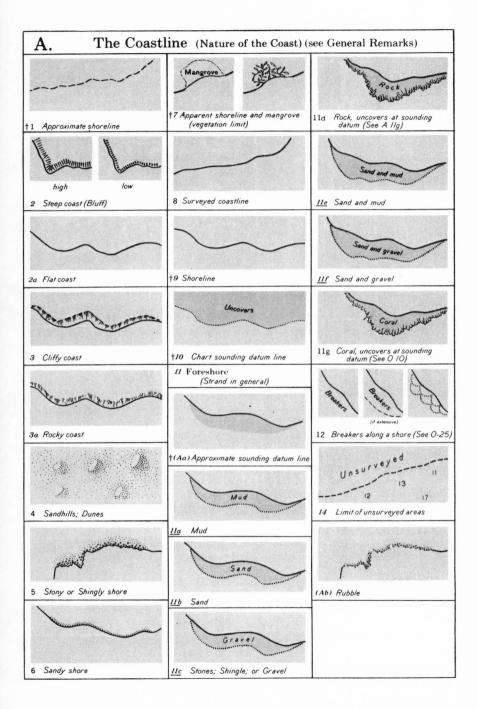

# A. The Coastline (Nature of the Coast) (see General Remarks)

†1 *Approximate shoreline*

†7 *Apparent shoreline and mangrove (vegetation limit)*

11d *Rock, uncovers at sounding datum (See A 11g)*

2 *Steep coast (Bluff)* — *high* — *low*

8 *Surveyed coastline*

*11e Sand and mud*

2a *Flat coast*

†9 *Shoreline*

*11f Sand and gravel*

3 *Cliffy coast*

†10 *Chart sounding datum line*

11g *Coral, uncovers at sounding datum (See O 10)*

3a *Rocky coast*

*11 Foreshore (Strand in general)*

12 *Breakers along a shore (See O-25)* — *(if extensive)*

4 *Sandhills; Dunes*

†(Aa) *Approximate sounding datum line*

14 *Limit of unsurveyed areas* — *Unsurveyed*

5 *Stony or Shingly shore*

*11a Mud*

6 *Sandy shore*

*11b Sand*

(Ab) *Rubble*

*11c Stones; Shingle; or Gravel*

# B. Coast Features

| 1 | G | Gulf |
|---|---|---|
| 2 | B | Bay |
| (Ba) | B | Bayou |
| 3 | Fd | Fjord |
| 4 | L | Loch; Lough; Lake |
| 5 | Cr | Creek |
| 5a | C | Cove |
| 6 | In | Inlet |
| 7 | Str | Strait |
| 8 | Sd | Sound |
| 9 | Pass / Thoro | Passage; Pass / Thorofare |
| 10 | Chan | Channel |
| 10a | | Narrows |
| 11 | Entr | Entrance |
| 12 | Est | Estuary |
| 12a | | Delta |
| 13 | Mth | Mouth |
| 14 | Rd | Road; Roadstead |
| 15 | Anch | Anchorage |
| 16 | Hbr | Harbor |
| 16a | Hn | Haven |
| 17 | P | Port |
| (Bb) | P | Pond |
| 18 | I | Island |
| 19 | It | Islet |
| 20 | Arch | Archipelago |
| 21 | Pen | Peninsula |
| 22 | C | Cape |
| 23 | Prom | Promontory |
| 24 | Hd | Head; Headland |
| 25 | Pt | Point |
| 26 | Mt | Mountain; Mount |
| 27 | Rge | Range |
| 27a | | Valley |
| 28 | | Summit |
| 29 | Pk | Peak |
| 30 | Vol | Volcano |
| 31 | | Hill |
| 32 | Bld | Boulder |
| 33 | Ldg | Landing |
| 34 | | Tableland (Plateau) |
| 35 | Rk | Rock |
| 36 | | Isolated rock |
| (Bc) | Str | Stream |
| (Bd) | R | River |
| (Be) | Slu | Slough |
| (Bf) | Lag | Lagoon |
| (Bg) | Apprs | Approaches |
| (Bh) | Rky | Rocky |
| †(Bi) | Is | Islands |
| †(Bj) | Ma | Marsh |
| †(Bk) | Mg | Mangrove |
| †(Bl) | Sw | Swamp |

# C. The Land (Natural Features)

1 Contour lines (Contours)

1a Contour lines, approximate (Contours)

2 Hachures

2a Form lines, no definite interval

2b Shading

3 Glacier

4 Saltpans

5 Isolated trees

5a Deciduous or of unknown or unspecified type

5b Coniferous

5c Palm tree

5d Nipa palm

5e Filao

5f Casuarina

5g Evergreen tree (other than coniferous)

6 Cultivated fields

6a Grass fields

7 Paddy (rice) fields

7a Park; Garden

8 Bushes

8a Tree plantation in general

9 Deciduous woodland

10 Coniferous woodland

10a Woods in general

11 Tree top height (above shoreline datum)

12 Lava flow

13 River; Stream

14 Intermittent stream

15 Lake; Pond

16 Lagoon (Lag)

17 Marsh; Swamp

Symbol used in small areas

18 Slough (Slu.)

19 Rapids

20 Waterfalls

21 Spring

# D. Control Points

| 1 | △ | | Triangulation point (station) |
|---|---|---|---|
| 1a | | | Astronomic station |
| 2 | ⊙ | (See In) | Fixed point (landmark, position accurate) |
| (Da) | ○ | (See Io) | Fixed point (landmark, position approx.) |
| 3 | · 256 | | Summit of height (Peak) (when not a landmark) |
| (Db) | ◎ 256 | | Peak, accentuated by contours |
| (Dc) | ※ 256 | | Peak, accentuated by hachures |
| (Dd) | ✹ | | Peak, elevation not determined |
| (De) | ⊙ 256 | | Peak, when a landmark |
| 4 | ⊕ | Obs Spot | Observation spot |
| *5 | | BM | Bench mark |
| 6 | View X | | View point |
| 7 | | | Datum point for grid of a plan |
| 8 | | | Graphical triangulation point |
| 9 | | Astro | Astronomical |
| 10 | | Tri | Triangulation |
| (Df) | | C of E | Corps of Engineers |
| 12 | | | Great trigonometrical survey station |
| 13 | | | Traverse station |
| 14 | | Bdy Mon | Boundary monument |
| (Dg) | ◇ | | International boundary monument |

# E. Units

| †1 | hr, h | Hour |
|---|---|---|
| †2 | m, min | Minute (of time) |
| †3 | sec, s | Second (of time) |
| 4 | m | Meter |
| 4a | dm | Decimeter |
| 4b | cm | Centimeter |
| 4c | mm | Millimeter |
| 4d | m² | Square meter |
| 4e | m³ | Cubic meter |
| 5 | km | Kilometer |
| 6 | in | Inch |
| 7 | ft | Foot |
| 8 | yd | Yard |
| 9 | fm | Fathom |
| 10 | cbl | Cable length |
| †11 | M, Mi, N Mi | Nautical mile |
| 12 | kn | Knot |
| †12a | t | Tonne (metric ton = 2,204.6 lbs.) |
| 12b | cd | Candela (new candle) |
| 13 | lat | Latitude |
| 14 | long | Longitude |
| 14a | | Greenwich |
| 15 | pub | Publication |
| 16 | Ed | Edition |
| 17 | corr | Correction |
| 18 | alt | Altitude |

| 19 | ht; elev | Height; Elevation |
|---|---|---|
| 20 | ° | Degree |
| 21 | ' | Minute (of arc) |
| 22 | " | Second (of arc) |
| 23 | No | Number |
| †(Ea) | St M, St Mi | Statute mile |
| †(Eb) | μsec, μs | Microsecond |
| (Ec) | Hz | Hertz (cps) |
| (Ed) | kHz | Kilohertz (kc) |
| (Ee) | MHz | Megahertz (Mc) |
| †(Ef) | cps, c/s | Cycles/second (Hz) |
| (Eg) | kc | Kilocycle (kHz) |
| (Eh) | Mc | Megacycle (MHz) |
| †(Ei) | T | Ton (U.S. short ton = 2,000 lbs.) |

# F. Adjectives, Adverbs, Nouns, and Other Words

| 1 | gt | Great |
|---|---|---|
| 2 | lit | Little |
| 3 | Lrg | Large |
| 4 | sml | Small |
| 5 | | Outer |
| 6 | | Inner |
| 7 | mid | Middle |
| 8 | | Old |
| 9 | anc | Ancient |
| 10 | | New |
| 11 | St | Saint |
| 12 | conspic | Conspicuous |
| 13 | | Remarkable |
| 14 | D, Destr | Destroyed |
| 15 | | Projected |
| 16 | dist | Distant |
| 17 | abt | About |
| 18 | | See chart |
| 18a | | See plan |
| 19 | | Lighted; Luminous |
| 20 | sub | Submarine |
| 21 | | Eventual |
| 22 | AERO | Aeronautical |
| 23 | | Higher |
| 23a | | Lower |
| 24 | exper | Experimental |
| 25 | discontd | Discontinued |
| 26 | prohib | Prohibited |
| 27 | explos | Explosive |
| 28 | estab | Established |
| 29 | elec | Electric |
| 30 | priv | Private, Privately |
| 31 | prom | Prominent |
| 32 | std | Standard |
| 33 | subm | Submerged |
| 34 | approx | Approximate |
| 35 | | Maritime |
| 36 | maintd | Maintained |
| 37 | aband | Abandoned |
| 38 | temp | Temporary |
| 39 | occas | Occasional |
| 40 | extr | Extreme |
| 41 | | Navigable |
| 42 | N M | Notice to Mariners |
| (Fa) | L N M | Local Notice to Mariners |
| 43 | | Sailing Directions |
| 44 | | List of Lights |
| (Fb) | unverd | Unverified |
| (Fc) | AUTH | Authorized |
| (Fd) | CL | Clearance |
| (Fe) | cor | Corner |
| (Ff) | concr | Concrete |
| (Fg) | fl | Flood |
| (Fh) | mod | Moderate |
| (Fi) | bet | Between |
| (Fj) | 1st | First |
| †(Fk) | 2nd, 2d | Second |
| †(Fl) | 3rd, 3d | Third |
| (Fm) | 4th | Fourth |
| (Fn) | DD | Deep Draft |
| (Fo) | min | Minimum |
| (Fp) | max | Maximum |
| †(Fq) | N'ly | Northerly |
| †(Fr) | S'ly | Southerly |
| †(Fs) | E'ly | Easterly |
| †(Ft) | W'ly | Westerly |
| †(Fu) | Sk | Stroke |
| †(Fv) | Restr | Restricted |

# G.        Ports and Harbors

| | | | |
|---|---|---|---|
| 1 | ⚓ | Anch | Anchorage (large vessels) |
| 2 | ⚓ ⚓ | Anch | Anchorage (small vessels) |
| 3 | | Hbr | Harbor |
| 4 | | Hn | Haven |
| 5 | | P | Port |
| 6 | | Bkw | Breakwater |
| 6a | | | Dike |
| 7 | | | Mole |
| 8 | | | Jetty (partly below MHW) |
| 8a | | | Submerged jetty |
| (Ga) | | | Jetty (small scale) |
| 9 | | Pier | Pier |
| 10 | | | Spit |
| 11 | | | Groin (partly below MHW) |
| 12 | ANCH PROHIBITED | ANCH PROHIB | Anchorage prohibited (screen optional)(See P 25) |
| 12a | | | Anchorage reserved |
| 12b | QUARANTINE ANCHORAGE | QUAR ANCH | Quarantine anchorage |
| 13 | Spoil Area | | Spoil ground |
| (Gb) | Dumping Ground | | Dumping ground |
| (Gc) | 80   83   85 Disposal Area depths from survey of JUNE 1972 90   98 | | Disposal area |
| (Gd) | | | Pump-out facilities |
| 14 | | Fsh stks | Fisheries, Fishing stakes |
| 14a | | | Fish trap; Fish weirs (actual shape charted) |
| 14b | | | Duck blind |
| 15 | | | Tuna nets (See G 14a) |
| 15a | Oys | Oys | Oyster bed |
| 16 | | Ldg | Landing place |
| 17 | | | Watering place |
| 18 | | Whf | Wharf |
| 19 | | | Quay |

| | | | |
|---|---|---|---|
| 20 | | | Berth |
| 20a | 14 | | Anchoring berth |
| 20b | 3 | | Berth number |
| 21 | • | Dol | Dolphin |
| 22 | | | Bollard |
| 23 | | | Mooring ring |
| 24 | ⊖ | | Crane |
| 25 | | | Landing stage |
| 25a | | | Landing stairs |
| 26 | ⊕ | Quar | Quarantine |
| 27 | | | Lazaret |
| *28 | | Harbor Master | Harbormaster's office |
| 29 | | Cus Ho | Customhouse |
| 30 | | | Fishing harbor |
| 31 | | | Winter harbor |
| 32 | | | Refuge harbor |
| 33 | | B Hbr | Boat harbor |
| 34 | | | Stranding harbor (uncovers at LW) |
| 35 | | | Dock |
| 36 | | | Drydock (actual shape on large-scale charts) |
| 37 | | | Floating dock (actual shape on large-scale charts) |
| 38 | | | Gridiron; Careening grid |
| 39 | | | Patent slip; Slipway; Marine railway |
| 39a | | Ramp | Ramp |
| 40 | Lock | | Lock (point upstream) (See H 13) |
| 41 | | | Wetdock |
| 42 | | | Shipyard |
| 43 | | | Lumber yard |
| 44 | ⊕ | Health Office | Health officer's office |
| 45 | ⟨⟩ | Hk | Hulk (actual shape on large-scale charts) (See O 11) |
| 46 | PROHIBITED AREA | PROHIB AREA | Prohibited area (screen optional) |
| 46a | 10 | | Calling-in point for vessel traffic control |
| 47 | | | Anchorage for seaplanes |
| 48 | | | Seaplane landing area |
| 49 | Under construction | | Work in progress |
| 50 | | | Under construction |
| 51 | | | Work projected |
| (Ge) | Subm ruins | | Submerged ruins |

# H.  Topography  (Artificial Features)

| | |
|---|---|
| 1  Road (Rd) or Highway (Hy)<br>*Small-scale chart* | 13  Canal, Ditch, Lock, Sluice (point upstream)<br>Canal → Lock<br>Ditch  Sluice  (Tidegate, Floodgate) |
| (Ha) Highway markers  (20) (50) (95) | 14  Bridge (BR) in general<br>*Small-scale chart* |
| 2  Track, Footpath, or Trail | 14a  Stone, concrete bridge (same as H 14) |
| 3  Railway (Ry) (single or double track); Railroad (RR)<br>M & L S RR<br>Same grade  Ry. above  Ry. below | 14b  Wooden bridge (same as H 14) |
| | 14c  Iron bridge (same as H 14) |
| 3a  Tramway | 14d  Suspension bridge (same as H 14) |
| 3b  Railway station | 15  Drawbridge (in general) |
| 3c  Tunnel (railroad or road) | 16  Swing bridge (same as H 15) |
| 3d  Embankment, Levee | 16a  Lift bridge |
| 3e  Cutting | |
| 3f  Causeway | 16b  Weighbridge or Bascule bridge |
| 4  Overhead power cable (OVHD PWR CAB)<br>OVERHEAD POWER CABLE AUTHORIZED CL 140 FT<br>TOWER  TOWER | 17  Pontoon bridge |
| 5  Power transmission line | 17a  Footbridge |
| 5a  Power transmission mast | 18  Transporter bridge (same as H 14) |
| 6  Prominent telegraph or telephone line  Tel | 18a  Bridge clearance, vertical  VERT CL 6 FT |
| 7  Aqueduct; Water pipe | 18b  Bridge clearance, horizontal  HOR CL 28 FT |
| 8  Viaduct  Viaduct | 19  Ferry (Fy)<br>Ferry  Ferry  On small-scale chart |
| 8a  Pipeline | (Hb)  Cable ferry  Cable ferry |
| 9  Pile; Piling; Post (generally above MHW)  (See H 9a, L 59, O 30)<br>° Pile  °° Piling  ° Post  Piling | 20  Ford |
| 9a  Pile; Piling; Post (above sounding datum)  (See H 9, L 59, O 30)<br>° Pile  °° Piling  ° Post | 21  Dam |
| 10  Highway (See H I) | 22  Fence |
| 11  Sewer  Sewer or Outfall | 23  Training wall |
| 12  Culvert | †24  Log boom  Log boom |

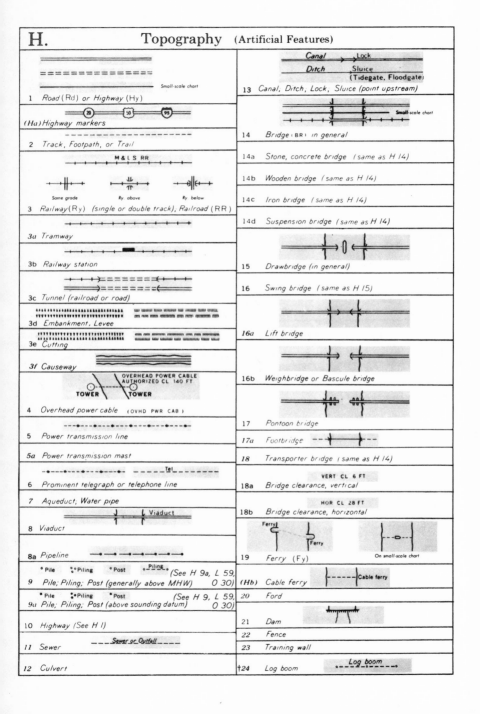

# I. Buildings and Structures (see General Remarks)

| | | | | | | | | |
|---|---|---|---|---|---|---|---|---|
| 1 | | | City or Town (large scale) | 26a | Locust Ave | | Ave | Avenue |
| (1a) | | | City or Town (small scale) | 26b | Grand Blvd | | Blvd | Boulevard |
| 2 | | | Suburb | 27 | | | Tel | Telegraph |
| 3 | | Vil | Village | 28 | | | Tel Off | Telegraph office |
| 3a | | | Buildings in general | 29 | | | PO | Post office |
| 4 | | Cas | Castle | 30 | | | Govt Ho | Government house |
| 5 | | | House | 31 | | | | Town hall |
| 6 | | | Villa | 32 | | | Hosp | Hospital |
| 7 | | | Farm | 33 | | | | Slaughterhouse |
| 8 | | | Church | 34 | | | Magz | Magazine |
| 8a | | Cath | Cathedral | 34a | | | | Warehouse; Storehouse |
| 8b | SPIRE | Spire | Spire; Steeple | 35 | MON | Mon | | Monument |
| 9 | | | Roman Catholic Church | 36 | CUP | Cup | | Cupola |
| 10 | | | Temple | 37 | ELEV | Elev | | Elevator; Lift |
| 11 | | | Chapel | (1e) | | | Elev | Elevation; Elevated |
| 12 | | | Mosque | 38 | | | | Shed |
| 12a | | | Minaret | 39 | | | | Zinc roof |
| (1b) | | | Moslem Shrine | 40 | Ruins | Ru | | Ruins |
| 13 | | | Marabout | 41 | TR | Tr | | Tower |
| 14 | | Pag | Pagoda | (1f) | ABAND LT HO | | | Abandoned lighthouse |
| 15 | | | Buddhist Temple; Joss-House | 42 | WINDMILL | | | Windmill |
| 15a | | | Shinto Shrine | 43 | | | | Watermill |
| 16 | | | Monastery; Convent | 43a | WINDMOTOR | | | Windmotor |
| 17 | | | Calvary; Cross | 44 | CHY | Chy | | Chimney; Stack |
| 17a | | | Cemetery, Non-Christian | 45 | S·PIPE | S'pipe | | Water tower; Standpipe |
| 18 | Cem | | Cemetery, Christian | 46 | | | | Oil tank |
| 18a | | | Tomb | 47 | Facty | | | Factory |
| 19 | | | Fort (actual shape charted) | 48 | | | | Saw mill |
| 20 | | | Battery | 49 | | | | Brick kiln |
| 21 | | | Barracks | 50 | | | | Mine; Quarry |
| 22 | | | Powder magazine | 51 | Well | | | Well |
| 23 | Airport | | Airplane landing field | 52 | | | | Cistern |
| 24 | | | Airport, large scale (See P-13) | 53 | TANK | Tk | | Tank |
| (1c) | | | Airport, military (small scale) | 54 | | | | Noria |
| (1d) | | | Airport, civil (small scale) | 55 | | | | Fountain |
| 25 | | | Mooring mast | | | | | |
| 26 | King St | St | Street | | | | | |

# I.     Buildings and Structures (continued)

| | | | | | | | | |
|---|---|---|---|---|---|---|---|---|
| 61 | | Inst | Institute | 72 | ⊙GAB | °Gab | | Gable |
| 62 | | | Establishment | 73 | | | | Wall |
| 63 | | | Bathing establishment | 74 | | | | Pyramid |
| 64 | | Ct Ho | Courthouse | 75 | | | | Pillar |
| 65 | | Sch | School | 76 | | | | Oil derrick |
| (Ig) | | HS | High school | (Ii) | | | Ltd | Limited |
| (Ih) | | Univ | University | (Ij) | | | Apt | Apartment |
| 66 | | Bldg | Building | (Ik) | | | Cap | Capitol |
| 67 | | Pav | Pavilion | (Il) | | | Co | Company |
| 68 | | | Hut | (Im) | | | Corp | Corporation |
| 69 | | | Stadium | (In) | ⊙ | | | Landmark (position accurate)(See D 2) |
| 70 | | T | Telephone | (Io) | o | | | Landmark (position approximate)(See Da) |
| 71 | | | Gas tank; Gasometer | | | | | |

# J.     Miscellaneous Stations

| | | | | | | | |
|---|---|---|---|---|---|---|---|
| 1 | | Sta | Any kind of station | 13 | | | Tide signal station |
| 2 | | Sta | Station | 14 | | | Stream signal station |
| 3 | | C G | Coast Guard station (similar to Lifesaving Station, J 6) | 15 | | | Ice signal station |
| | | | | 16 | | | Time signal station |
| (Ja) | | R TR C G WALLIS SANDS | Coast Guard station (when landmark) | 16a | | | Manned oceanographic station |
| | | | | 16b | | | Unmanned oceanographic station |
| 4 | | ⊙ LOOK TR | Lookout station; Watch tower | 17 | | | Time ball |
| 5 | | | Lifeboat station | 18 | | | Signal mast |
| 6 | | LS S | Lifesaving station (See J 3) | †18a | °Mast | | Mast |
| | | | | 19 | °FS °FS ⊙FP °FP | | Flagstaff; Flagpole |
| 7 | | Rkt Sta | Rocket station | 19a | ⊙F TR °FTr | | Flag tower |
| 8 | | ⊙ PIL STA | Pilot station | 20 | | | Signal |
| 9 | | Sig Sta | Signal station | 21 | | Obsy | Observatory |
| 10 | | Sem | Semaphore | 22 | | Off | Office |
| 11 | | S Sig Sta | Storm signal station | (Jc) | °BELL | | Bell (on land) |
| 12 | | | Weather signal station | (Jd) | °HECP | | Harbor entrance control post |
| (Jb) | ⊙NWS SIG STA | | Nat'l Weather Service signal sta | †(Je) | °MARINE POLICE | | Marine police station |
| | | | | †(Jf) | °FIREBOAT STATION | | Fireboat station |

# K. Lights

| No. | Symbol | Description | No. | Symbol | Description |
|---|---|---|---|---|---|
| 1 | | Position of light | 29 | F Fl | Fixed and flashing light |
| 2 | Lt | Light | 30 | F Gp Fl | Fixed and group flashing light |
| (Ka) | | Riprap surrounding light | 30a | Mo | Morse code light |
| 3 | Lt Ho | Lighthouse | 31 | Rot | Revolving or Rotating light |
| 4 | AERO | Aeronautical light (See F-22) | 41 | | Period |
| 4a | | Marine and air navigation light | 42 | | Every |
| 5 | Bn | Light beacon | 43 | | With |
| 6 | | Light vessel; Lightship | 44 | | Visible (range) |
| 8 | | Lantern | †(Kb) | M; Mi; N Mi | Nautical mile (See E-11) |
| 9 | | Street lamp | (Kc) | m min | Minutes (See E-2) |
| 10 | REF | Reflector | †(Kd) | s; sec | Seconds (See E-3) |
| 11 | Ldg Lt | Ldg Lt Leading light | 45 | Fl | Flash |
| 12 | RED | Sector light | 46 | Occ | Occultation |
| 13 | GREEN RED | Directional light | 46a | | Eclipse |
| | | | 47 | Gp | Group |
| 14 | | Harbor light | 48 | Occ | Intermittent light |
| 15 | | Fishing light | | | |
| 16 | | Tidal light | 49 | SEC | Sector |
| 17 | Priv maintd | Private light (maintained by private interests; to be used with caution) | 50 | | Color of sector |
| 21 | F | Fixed light | 51 | Aux | Auxiliary light |
| 22 | Occ | Occulting light | 52 | | Varied |
| 23 | Fl | Flashing light | 61 | Vi | Violet |
| 23a | Iso E Int | Isophase light (equal interval) | 62 | | Purple |
| 24 | Qk Fl | Quick flashing (scintillating) light | 63 | B | Blue |
| 25 | Int Qk Fl I Qk Fl | Interrupted quick flashing light | 64 | G | Green |
| | | | 65 | Or | Orange |
| 25a | S Fl | Short flashing light | 66 | R | Red |
| 26 | Alt | Alternating light | 67 | W | White |
| 27 | Gp Occ | Group occulting light | 67a | Am | Amber |
| 28 | Gp Fl | Group flashing light | 67b | Y | Yellow |
| 28a | S-L Fl | Short-long flashing light | 68 | OBSC | Obscured light |
| 28b | | Group short flashing light | 68a | Fog Det Lt | Fog detector light (See Nb) |

| | | | | | | |
|---|---|---|---|---|---|---|
| 69 | | Unwatched light | 79 | | Front light |
| 70 | Occas | Occasional light | 80 | Vert | Vertical lights |
| 71 | Irreg | Irregular light | 81 | Hor | Horizontal lights |
| 72 | Prov | Provisional light | (Kf) | VB | Vertical beam |
| 73 | Temp | Temporary light | (Kg) | RGE | Range |
| (Ke) | D: Destr | Destroyed | (Kh) | Exper | Experimental light |
| 74 | Exting | Extinguished light | (Ki) | TRLB | Temporarily replaced by lighted buoy showing the same characteristics |
| 75 | | Faint light | | | |
| 76 | | Upper light | (Kj) | TRUB | Temporarily replaced by unlighted buoy |
| 77 | | Lower light | (Kk) | TLB | Temporary lighted buoy |
| 78 | | Rear light | (Kl) | TUB | Temporary unlighted buoy |

## L.    Buoys and Beacons
### (see General Remarks)

† ( ♂♂♂♂♂♂♂♂♂♂ new standard symbols)

| | | | | | |
|---|---|---|---|---|---|
| 1 | | Approximate position of buoy | †17 | RB RB RB | Bifurcation buoy (RBHB) |
| †2 | | Light buoy | †18 | RB RB RB | Junction buoy (RBHB) |
| †3 | BELL BELL BELL | Bell buoy | †19 | RB RB RB | Isolated danger buoy (RBHB) |
| †3a | GONG GONG GONG | Gong buoy | †20 | RB RB / G G G G | Wreck buoy (RBHB or G) |
| †4 | WHIS WHIS | Whistle buoy | †20a | RB RB / G G | Obstruction buoy (RBHB or G) |
| †5 | C C | Can or Cylindrical buoy | †21 | Tel Tel | Telegraph-cable buoy |
| †6 | N N | Nun or Conical buoy | 22 | | Mooring buoy (colors of mooring buoys never carried) |
| †7 | SP SP | Spherical buoy | 22a | | Mooring |
| †8 | S S | Spar buoy | 22b | Tel Tel | Mooring buoy with telegraphic communications |
| †8a | P P | Pillar or Spindle buoy | 22c | T T | Mooring buoy with telephonic communications |
| †9 | | Buoy with topmark (ball) (see L-70) | †23 | | Warping buoy |
| †10 | | Barrel or Ton buoy | †24 | Y Y | Quarantine buoy |
| †(La) | | Color unknown | 24a | | Practice area buoy |
| †(Lb) | FLOAT FLOAT | Float | †25 | Explos Anch Explos Anch | Explosive anchorage buoy |
| †12 | FLOAT FLOAT FLOAT | Lightfloat | †25a | AERO AERO | Aeronautical anchorage buoy |
| 13 | | Outer or Landfall buoy | †26 | Deviation Deviation | Compass adjustment buoy |
| †14 | BW BW | Fairway buoy (BWVS) | †27 | BW BW | Fish trap (area) buoy (BWHB) |
| †14a | BW BW | Midchannel buoy (BWVS) | †27a | | Spoil ground buoy |
| †15 | R "2" R "2" R "2" | Starboard-hand buoy (entering from seaward) | †28 | W W | Anchorage buoy (marks limits) |
| †16 | "1" "1" | Port-hand buoy (entering from seaward) | †29 | Priv maintd Priv maintd | Private aid to navigation (buoy) (maintained by private interests, use with caution) |

| | | | | | | |
|---|---|---|---|---|---|---|
| 29 (cont.) | ! | R | Starboard-hand buoy (entering from seaward) | | | |
| | ! | B | Port-hand buoy | 55 | | Cardinal marking system |
| 30 | | | Temporary buoy (See Ki, j, k, l) | 56 | △ Deviation Bn | Compass adjustment beacon |
| 30a | | | Winter buoy | | | |
| †31 | | | Horozontal stripes or bands HB | 57 | | Topmarks (See L 9, 70) |
| †32 | | | Vertical stripes VS | 58 | | Telegraph-cable (landing) beacon |
| †33 | | | Checkered Chec | 59 | Piles  Piles | Piles (See O 30; H 9, 9a) |
| †33a | | Diag | Diagonal bands | | ⊥⊥ Stakes | Stakes |
| 41 | ☐ | W | White | | Stumps | Stumps (See O 30) |
| 42 | ■ | B | Black | | ⊥⊥ Perches | Perches |
| 43 | ▨ | R | Red | | | |
| 44 | ▦ | Y | Yellow | 61 | ⊙ CAIRN   ° Cairn | Cairn |
| 45 | ▨ | G | Green | 62 | | Painted patches |
| 46 | | Br | Brown | 63 | ⊙ TR | Landmark (position accurate) (See D 2) |
| 47 | | Gy | Gray | (Ld) | ° Tr | Landmark (position approximate) |
| 48 | ▤ | Bu | Blue | 64 | REF | Reflector |
| 48a | | Am | Amber | 65 | ⊙ MARKER | Range targets, markers |
| 48b | | Or | Orange | †(Le) | W Or  W Or  W Or  W Or | Special-purpose buoys |
| | | | | 66 | | Oil installation buoy |
| †51 | | | Floating beacon | 67 | | Drilling platform (See Of, Og) |
| 52 | △RW Bn  △W Bn  △R Bn | | Fixed beacon (unlighted or daybeacon) | 70 | Note: | TOPMARKS on buoys and beacons may be shown on charts of foreign waters. The abbreviation for black is not shown adjacent to buoys or beacons. |
| | ▲ Bn | | Black beacon | | | |
| | △ Bn | | Color unknown | | | |
| (Lc) | ⊙ MARKER  ° Marker | | Private aid to navigation | (Lf) | Ra Ref | Radar reflector (See M 13) |
| 53 | | Bn | Beacon, in general (See L 52) | | | |
| 54 | | | Tower beacon | | | |

# M. Radio and Radar Stations

| | | | | | | |
|---|---|---|---|---|---|---|
| 1 | ° R Sta | Radio telegraph station | 12 | (⊙) Racon | Radar responder beacon |
| 2 | ° RT | Radio telephone station | 13 | Ra Ref | Radar reflector (See L-Lf) |
| 3 | (⊙) R Bn | Radiobeacon | 14 | Ra (conspic) | Radar conspicuous object |
| 4 | (⊙) R Bn | Circular radiobeacon | 14a | | Ramark |
| 5 | (⊙) RD | Directional radiobeacon; Radio range | 15 | D F S | Distance finding station (synchronized signals) |
| 6 | | Rotating loop radiobeacon | 16 | (⊙) AERO R Bn 302 | Aeronautical radiobeacon |
| 7 | (⊙) RDF | Radio direction finding station | 17 | ° Decca Sta | Decca station |
| †(Ma) | ANTENNA (TELEM) TELEM ANT | Telemetry antenna | 18 | ° Loran Sta Venice | Loran station (name) |
| (Mb) | ° R RELAY MAST | Radio relay mast | 19 | (⊙) CONSOL Bn 190 kHz MMF | Consol (Consolan) station |
| (Mc) | ° MICRO TR | Microwave tower | (Md) | (⊙) AERO R Rge 342 | Aeronautical radio range |
| 9 | ° R MAST / ° R TR | Radio mast / Radio tower | (Me) | (⊙) Ra Ref Calibration Bn | Radar calibration beacon |
| 9a | ° TV TR | Television mast; Television tower | (Mf) | ° LORAN TR SPRING ISLAND | Loran tower (name) |
| 10 | ° R TR (WBAL) 1090 KHZ | Radio broadcasting station (commercial) | (Mg) | ° R TR F R Lt | Obstruction light |
| 10a | ° R Sta | QTG radio station | †(Mh) | ° RA DOME ° DOME (RADAR) ° Ra Dome ° Dome (Radar) | Radar dome |
| 11 | (⊙) Ra | Radar station | †(Mi) | uhf | Ultrahigh frequency |
| | | | †(Mj) | vhf | Very high frequency |

# N. Fog Signals

| | | | | | | |
|---|---|---|---|---|---|---|
| 1 | Fog Sig | Fog-signal station | 13 | HORN | Foghorn |
| 2 | | Radio fog-signal station | 13a | HORN | Electric foghorn |
| 3 | GUN | Explosive fog signal | 14 | BELL | Fog bell |
| 4 | | Submarine fog signal | 15 | WHIS | Fog whistle |
| 5 | SUB-BELL | Submarine fog bell (action of waves) | 16 | HORN | Reed horn |
| 6 | SUB-BELL | Submarine fog bell (mechanical) | 17 | GONG | Fog gong |
| 7 | SUB-OSC | Submarine oscillator | 18 | ⊙ | Submarine sound signal not connected to the shore (See N 5,6,7) |
| 8 | NAUTO | Nautophone | 18a | ⊙vvvv | Submarine sound signal connected to the shore (See N 5,6,7) |
| 9 | DIA | Diaphone | | | |
| 10 | GUN | Fog gun | (Na) | HORN | Typhon |
| 11 | SIREN | Fog siren | (Nb) | Fog Det Lt | Fog detector light (See K 68a) |
| 12 | HORN | Fog trumpet | | | |

# O.    Dangers

1 Rock which does not cover
(height above MHW)
(See General Remarks)

*Uncov 2 ft*    *Uncov 2 ft*

* (2)    (2)

†2 Rock which covers and uncovers,
with height above chart sounding datum

3 Rock awash at (near) level of
chart sounding datum

Dotted line emphasizes danger to
navigation

(Oa) Rock awash (height unknown)

Dotted line emphasizes danger to
navigation

4 Submerged rock (depth unknown)

Dotted line emphasizes danger to
navigation

*Rk*

5 Shoal sounding on isolated rock

6 Submerged rock not dangerous
to surface navigation (See O 4)

*Rk*    *Wk*    *Obstr*

6a Sunken danger with depth cleared
by wire drag (in feet or fathoms)

*Reef*

7 Reef of unknown extent

*Sub Vol*

8 Submarine volcano

*Discol Water*

9 Discolored water

*Co*    *Co*

10 Coral reef, detached (uncovers at
sounding datum)

Coral or Rocky reef, covered at
sounding datum (See A-11d, 11g)

---

11 Wreck showing any portion of hull or
superstructure (above sounding datum)

*Masts*

12 Wreck with only masts visible
(above sounding datum)

13 Old symbols for wrecks

*PA (position approx)*

†13a Wreck always partially submerged

14 Sunken wreck dangerous to surface
navigation (less than 11 fathoms
over wreck) (See O 6a)

*Wk*

15 Wreck over which depth is known

*Wk*

15a Wreck with depth cleared by
wire drag

*Wk*

†15b Unsurveyed wreck over which the
exact depth is unknown, but is
considered to have a safe
clearance to the depth shown

16 Sunken wreck, not dangerous to
surface navigation

*Foul*

†17 Foul ground, Foul bottom (fb)

*Tide Rips*

18 Overfalls or        Symbol used only
Tide rips           in small areas

*Eddies*              Symbol used only
19 Eddies              in small areas

*Kelp*                Symbol used only
20 Kelp, Seaweed      in small areas

21 Bk    Bank
22 Shl   Shoal
23 Rf    Reef (See A 11d, 11g, O 10)
23a      Ridge
24 Le    Ledge

25 Breakers (See A 12)

26 Submerged rock (See O 4)

*Obstr*

27 Obstruction

†(Ob) *Obstr*  *Well*   Subm well
      *Obstr*  *Well*   Subm well
                        (buoyed)

---

*Obstruction
(Fish haven)*

(Oc) Fish haven (artificial fishing reef)

28 Wreck (See O 11 to 16)

*Wreckage*    *Wks*

29 Wreckage

29a Wreck remains (dangerous
only for anchoring)

*Subm piles*    *Subm piling*

†30 Submerged piling
(See H-9, 9a; L 59)

*Snags*    *Stumps*

30a Snags; Submerged stumps
(See L 59)

31 Lesser depth possible

32 Uncov Dries (See A 10; O 2, 10)
33 Cov   Covers (See O 2, 10)
34 Uncov Uncovers
(See A 10; O 2, 10)

*(3) Rep (1958)*

Reported (with date)

*Eagle Rk
(rep 1958)*

35 Reported (with name and date)

36 Discol Discolored (See O 9)
37 Isolated danger

38 Limiting danger line

*rky.*

39 Limit of rocky area

41 P A    Position approximate
42 P D    Position doubtful
43 E D    Existence doubtful
44 P Pos  Position
45 D      Doubtful
46        Unexamined
(Od) L D  Least Depth

*Subm    Crib
Crib     (above water)*

(Oe) Crib

□ ■ Platform (lighted)
HORN

(Of) Offshore platform (unnamed)

□ ■ Hazel (lighted)
HORN

(Og) Offshore platform (named)

# P. Various Limits, etc.

| | | | | | |
|---|---|---|---|---|---|
| 1 | | Leading line; Range Line | 13a | | Limit of military practice areas |
| 2 | | Transit | 14 | | Limit of sovereignty (Territorial waters) |
| 3 | | In line with | 15 | | Customs boundary |
| 4 | | Limit of sector | 16 | | International boundary (also State boundary) |
| 5 | | Channel, Course, Track recommended (marked by buoys or beacons) (See P 21) | 17 | | Stream limit |
| | | | 18 | | Ice limit |
| (Pa) | | Alternate course | 19 | | Limit of tide |
| 6 | —Ra—Ra— | Radar-guided track | 20 | | Limit of navigation |
| 7 | | Submarine cable (power, telegraph, telephone, etc.) | 21 | | Course of recommended (not marked by buoys or beacons) (See P 5) |
| 7a | Cable Area | Submarine cable area | | | District or province limit |
| 7b | | Abandoned submarine cable (includes disused cable) | 23 | | Reservation line |
| 8 | | Submarine pipeline | | | (Options) |
| 8a | Pipeline Area | Submarine pipeline area | 24 | COURSE 053°00" TRUE  MARKERS | Measured distance |
| †8b | | Abandoned submarine pipeline | | | |
| 9 | | Maritime limit in general | 25 | PROHIBITED AREA | Prohibited area (See G 12, 46) (Screen optional) |
| (Pb) | RESTRICTED AREA | Limit of restricted area | (Pd) | SAFETY FAIRWAY | Shipping safety fairway |
| 10 | | Limit of fishing zone (fish trap areas) | | | |
| (Pc) | | U.S. Harbor Line | (Pe) | | Directed traffic lanes |
| 11 | | Limit of dumping ground, spoil ground (See P 9; G 13) | | | |
| 12 | | Anchorage limit | | | |
| 13 | | Limit of airport (See I 23, 24) | | | |

# Q. Soundings

| | | | | | | |
|---|---|---|---|---|---|---|
| 1 | SD | Doubtful sounding | 10 | | | Hairline depth figures |
| 2 | 65 | No bottom found | 10a | 8₂ | 19 | Figures for ordinary soundings |
| 3 | | Out of position | 11 | | | Soundings taken from foreign charts |
| 4 | | Least depth in narrow channels | | | | |
| 5 | 30 FEET APR 1972 | Dredged channel (with controlling depth indicated) | 12 | 8, | 19 | Soundings taken from older surveys (or smaller scale chts) |
| 6 | 24 FEET MAY 1972 | Dredged area | 13 | 8₂ | 19 | Echo soundings |
| 7 | | Swept channel (See Q 9) | 14 | 8, | 19 | Sloping figures (See Q 12) |
| †8 | | Drying (or uncovering) heights above chart sounding datum | 15 | 8₂ | 19 | Upright figures (See Q 10a) |
| | | | 16 | (25) | (2) | Bracketed figures (See O 1, 2) |
| 9 | 17 119 | Swept area, not adequately sounded (shown by green tint) | 17 | | | Underlined sounding figures (See Q 8) |
| | | | 18 | 3₂ | 6, | Soundings expressed in fathoms and feet |
| 9a | 29 23 3 22 8 30 18 21 7 | Swept area adequately sounded (swept by wire drag to depth indicated) | 22 | | | Unsounded area |
| | | | (Qa) | 6 5 21 | | Stream |

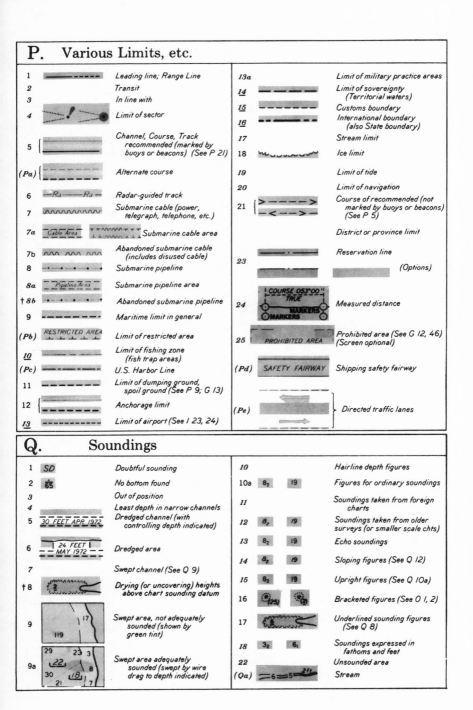

# R. Depth Contours and Tints (see General Remarks)

| Feet | Fm / Meters | | Feet | Fm / Meters | |
|------|-------------|--|------|-------------|--|
| 0 | 0 | | 300 | 50 | |
| 6 | 1 | | 600 | 100 | |
| 12 | 2 | | 1,200 | 200 | |
| 18 | 3 | | 1,800 | 300 | |
| 24 | 4 | | 2,400 | 400 | |
| 30 | 5 | | 3,000 | 500 | |
| 36 | 6 | | 6,000 | 1,000 | |
| 60 | 10 | | 12,000 | 2,000 | |
| 120 | 20 | | 18,000 | 3,000 | |
| 180 | 30 | | Or continuous lines, with values | | (blue or black) 5 — 100 |
| 240 | 40 | | | | |

# S. Quality of the Bottom

| 1 | Grd | Ground | 24 | Oys | Oysters | 50 | spk | Speckled |
|---|-----|--------|----|-----|---------|----|-----|----------|
| 2 | S | Sand | 25 | Ms | Mussels | 51 | gty | Gritty |
| 3 | M | Mud; Muddy | 26 | Spg | Sponge | 52 | dec | Decayed |
| 4 | Oz | Ooze | 27 | K | Kelp | 53 | fly | Flinty |
| 5 | Ml | Marl | 28 | Wd | Seaweed | 54 | glac | Glacial |
| 6 | Cl | Clay | 28 | Grs | Grass | 55 | ten | Tenacious |
| 7 | G | Gravel | 29 | Stg | Sea-tangle | 56 | wh | White |
| 8 | Sn | Shingle | 31 | Spi | Spicules | 57 | bk | Black |
| 9 | P | Pebbles | 32 | Fr | Foraminifera | 58 | vi | Violet |
| 10 | St | Stones | 33 | Gl | Globigerina | 59 | bu | Blue |
| 11 | Rk; rky | Rock; Rocky | 34 | Di | Diatoms | 60 | gn | Green |
| 11a | Blds | Boulders | 35 | Rd | Radiolaria | 61 | yl | Yellow |
| 12 | Ck | Chalk | 36 | Pt | Pteropods | 62 | or | Orange |
| 12a | Ca | Calcareous | 37 | Po | Polyzoa | 63 | rd | Red |
| 13 | Qz | Quartz | 38 | Cir | Cirripedia | 64 | br | Brown |
| 13a | Sch | Schist | 38a | Fu | Fucus | 65 | ch | Chocolate |
| 14 | Co | Coral | 38b | Ma | Mattes | 66 | gy | Gray |
| (Sa) | Co Hd | Coral head | 39 | fne | Fine | 67 | lt | Light |
| 15 | Mds | Madrepores | 40 | crs | Coarse | 68 | dk | Dark |
| 16 | Vol | Volcanic | 41 | sft | Soft | | | |
| (Sb) | Vol Ash | Volcanic ash | 42 | hrd | Hard | 70 | vard | Varied |
| 17 | La | Lava | 43 | stf | Stiff | 71 | unev | Uneven |
| 18 | Pm | Pumice | 44 | sml | Small | (Sc) | S/M | Surface layer and Under layer |
| 19 | T | Tufa | 45 | lrg | Large | | | |
| 20 | Sc | Scoriae | 46 | stk | Sticky | | | |
| 21 | Cn | Cinders | 47 | brk | Broken | | | |
| 21a | | Ash | 47a | grd | Ground (Shells) | 76 | | Freshwater springs in seabed |
| 22 | Mn | Manganese | 48 | rt | Rotten | | | |
| 23 | Sh | Shells | 49 | str | Streaky | | | |

# T.  Tides and Currents

| 1 | HW | High water |
|---|---|---|
| 1a | HHW | Higher high water |
| 2 | LW | Low water |
| (Ta) | LWD | Low-water datum |
| 2a | LLW | Lower low water |
| 3 | MTL | Mean tide level |
| 4 | MSL | Mean sea level |
| 4a | | Elevation of mean sea level above chart (sounding) datum |
| 5 | | Chart datum (datum for sounding reduction) |
| 6 | Sp | Spring tide |
| 7 | Np | Neap tide |
| 7a | MHW | Mean high water |
| 8 | MHWS | Mean high-water springs |
| 8a | MHWN | Mean high-water neaps |
| 8b | MHHW | Mean higher high water |
| 8c | MLW | Mean low water |
| 9 | MLWS | Mean low-water springs |
| 9a | MLWN | Mean low-water neaps |
| 9b | MLLW | Mean lower low water |
| 10 | ISLW | Indian spring low water |
| 11 | | High-water full and change (vulgar establishment of the port) |
| 12 | | Low-water full and change |
| 13 | | Mean establishment of the port |
| 13a | | Establishment of the port |
| 14 | | Unit of height |
| 15 | | Equinoctial |
| 16 | | Quarter; Quadrature |
| 17 | Str | Stream |
| 18 | ⟶2kn⟶ | Current, general, with rate |
| 19 | ⟶2 kn⟶ | Flood stream (current) with rate |
| 20 | ⟶2 kn⟶ | Ebb stream (current) with rate |
| 21 | ○Tide gauge | Tide gauge; Tidepole; Automatic tide gauge |
| 23 | vel | Velocity; Rate |
| 24 | kn | Knots |
| 25 | ht | Height |
| 26 | | Tide |
| 27 | | New moon |
| 28 | | Full moon |
| 29 | | Ordinary |
| 30 | | Syzygy |
| 31 | fl | Flood |
| 32 | | Ebb |
| 33 | | Tidal stream diagram |
| 34 | ◈ ◈ | Place for which tabulated tidal stream data are given |
| 35 | | Range (of tide) |
| 36 | | Phase lag |
| (Tb) | | Current diagram, with explanatory note |

# U.  Compass

### Compass Rose

The outer circle is in degrees with zero at true north. The inner circles are in points and degrees with the arrow indicating magnetic north.

| 1 | N | North |
|---|---|---|
| 2 | E | East |
| 3 | S | South |
| 4 | W | West |
| 5 | NE | Northeast |
| 6 | SE | Southeast |
| 7 | SW | Southwest |
| 8 | NW | Northwest |
| 9 | N | Northern |
| 10 | E | Eastern |
| 11 | S | Southern |
| 12 | W | Western |
| 21 | brg | Bearing |
| 22 | T | True |
| 23 | mag | Magnetic |
| 24 | var | Variation |
| 25 | | Annual change |
| 25a | | Annual change nil |
| 26 | | Abnormal variation; Magnetic attraction |
| 27 | deg | Degrees (See E-20) |
| 28 | dev | Deviation |

# Index of Abbreviations

## Abbreviations

| | | |
|---|---|---|
| Explos Anch | Explosive Anchorage (buoy) | L 25 |
| Exting | Extinguished (light) | K 74 |
| extr | Extreme | F 40 |

### F

| | | |
|---|---|---|
| F | Fixed (light) | K 21 |
| Facty | Factory | I 47 |
| Fd | Fjord | B 3 |
| F Fl | Fixed and flashing (light) | K 29 |
| F Gp Fl | Fixed and group flashing (light) | K 30 |
| Fl | Flash, Flashing (light) | K 23, 45 |
| fl | Flood | Fg; T 31 |
| fly | Flinty | S 53 |
| fm | Fathom | E 9 |
| fne | Fine | S 39 |
| Fog Det Lt | Fog detector light | K 68a; Nb |
| Fog Sig | Fog signal station | N 1 |
| FP | Flagpole | J 19 |
| Fr | Foraminifera | S 32 |
| FS | Flagstaff | J 19 |
| Fsh stks | Fishing stakes | G 14 |
| ft | Foot | E 7 |
| Ft | Fort | I 19 |
| F TR | Flag tower | J 19a |
| Fu | Fucus | S 38a |
| Fy | Ferry | H 19 |

### G

| | | |
|---|---|---|
| G | Gulf | B 1 |
| G | Gravel | S 7 |
| G, Gn, gn | Green | K 64; L 20, 20a, 45; S 60 |
| GAB | Gable | I 72 |
| Gl | Globigerina | S 33 |
| glac | Glacial | S 54 |
| GONG | Fog gong | N 17 |
| Govt Ho | Government House | I 30 |
| Gp | Group | K 47 |
| Gp Fl | Group flashing | K 28 |
| Gp Occ | Group occulting | K 27 |
| Grd, grd | Ground | S 1, 47a |
| Grs | Grass | S 28 |
| gt | Great | F 1 |
| gty | Gritty | S 51 |
| GUN | Explosive fog signal | N 3 |
| GUN | Fog gun | N 10 |
| Gy, gy | Gray | L 47; S 66 |

### H

| | | |
|---|---|---|
| HB | Horizontal bands or stripes | L 31 |
| Hbr | Harbor | B 16; G 3 |
| Hd | Head, Headland | B 24 |
| HECP | Harbor entrance control post | Jd |
| Hk | Hulk | G 45 |
| HHW | Higher high water | T la |
| Hn | Haven | B 16a; G 4 |
| Hor | Horizontal lights | K 81 |
| HOR CL | Horizontal clearance | H 18b |
| HORN | Fog trumpet, Foghorn, Reed horn, Typhon | N 12, 13, 13a, 16, Na |
| Hosp | Hospital | I 32 |
| hr, h | Hour | E 1 |
| hrd | Hard | S 42 |
| H S | High School | Ig |
| ht | Height | E 19; T 25 |
| HW | High water | T 1 |
| Hy | Highway | H 1 |
| Hz | Hertz | Ec |

### I

| | | |
|---|---|---|
| I | Island | B 18 |
| I Qk, Int Qk | Interrupted quick | K 25 |
| in | Inch | E 6 |
| In | Inlet | B 6 |
| Inst | Institute | I 61 |
| Irreg | Irregular | K 71 |
| ISLW | Indian spring low water | T 10 |
| Is | Islands | Bi |
| Iso | Isophase | K 23a |
| It | Islet | B 19 |

### K

| | | |
|---|---|---|
| K | Kelp | S 27 |
| kc | Kilocycle | Eg |
| kHz | Kilohertz | Ed |
| km | Kilometer | E 5 |
| kn | Knots | E 12; T 24 |

### L

| | | |
|---|---|---|
| L | Loch, Lough, Lake | B 4 |
| La | Lava | S 17 |
| Lag | Lagoon | Bf; C 16 |
| lat | Latitude | E 13 |
| LD | Least Depth | Od |
| Ldg | Landing, Landing place | B 33; G 16 |
| Ldg Lt | Leading light | K 11 |
| Le | Ledge | O 24 |
| Lit | Little | F 2 |
| LLW | Lower low water | T 2a |
| LNM | Local Notice to Mariners | Fa |
| long | Longitude | E 14 |
| LOOK TR | Lookout station, Watch tower | J 4 |
| lrg | Large | F 3; S 45 |
| LS S | Lifesaving station | J 6 |
| Lt | Light | K 2 |
| lt | Light | S 67 |
| Ltd | Limited | Ii |
| Lt Ho | Lighthouse | K 3 |
| LW | Low water | T 2 |
| LWD | Low water datum | Ta |

### M

| | | |
|---|---|---|
| M, Mi | Nautical mile | E11; Kb |
| M | Mud, Muddy | S 3 |
| m | Meter | E 4, d, e |
| $m^2$ | Square meter | E4d |
| $m^3$ | Cubic meter | E4c |
| m, min | Minute (of time) | E2; Kc |
| Ma | Marsh | Bj |
| Ma | Mattes | S 38b |
| mag | Magnetic | U 23 |
| Magz | Magazine | I 34 |
| maintd | Maintained | F 36 |
| max | Maximum | Fp |
| Mc | Megacycle | Eh |
| Mds | Madrepores | S 15 |

# Abbreviations

| | | | | | |
|---|---|---|---|---|---|
| Mg | Mangrove | Bk | Pag | Pagoda | I 14 |
| MHHW | Mean higher high water | T 8b | Pass | Passage, Pass | B 9 |
| MHW | Mean high water | T 7a | Pav | Pavilion | I 67 |
| MHWN | Mean high-water neaps | T 8a | PD | Position doubtful | O 42 |
| MHWS | Mean high-water springs | T 8 | Pen | Peninsula | B 21 |
| MHz | Megahertz | Ee | PIL STA | Pilot station | J 8 |
| MICRO TR | Microwave tower | Mc | Pk | Peak | B 29 |
| mid | Middle | F 7 | Pm | Pumice | S 18 |
| min | Minimum | Fo | Po | Polyzoa | S 37 |
| Mkr | Marker | Lc | P O | Post Office | I 29 |
| Ml | Marl | S 5 | P, Pos | Position | O 44 |
| MLLW | Mean lower low water | T 9b | priv | Private, Privately | F 30 |
| MLW | Mean low water | T 8c | Priv maintd | Privately maintained | K 17; L 29 |
| MLWN | Mean low-water neaps | T 9a | Prohib | Prohibited | F 26 |
| MLWS | Mean low-water springs | T 9 | prom | Prominent | F 31 |
| mm | Millimeter | E 4c | Prom | Promontory | B 23 |
| Mn | Manganese | S 22 | Prov | Provisional (light) | K 72 |
| Mo | Morse code light | K 30a | Pt | Point | B 25 |
| mod | Moderate | Fh | Pt | Pteropods | S 36 |
| MON | Monument | I 35 | pub | Publication | E 15 |
| Ms | Mussels | S 25 | P F | Pump-out facilities | Gd |
| μsec, μs | Microsecond (one millionth) | Eb | PWI | Potable water intake | |
| MSL | Mean sea level | T 4 | | | |
| Mt | Mountain, Mount | B 26 | **Q** | | |
| Mth | Mouth | B 13 | Quar | Quarantine | G 26 |
| MTL | Mean tide level | T 3 | Qk Fl | Quick flashing (light) | K 24 |
| **N** | | | Qz | Quartz | S 13 |
| N | North; Northern | U 1, 9 | **R** | | |
| N | Nun; Conical (buoy) | L 6 | R | Red | K 66; L 15, 43 |
| N M, N Mi | Nautical mile | E 11 | R | River | Bd |
| NAUTO | Nautophone | N 8 | Ra | Radar station | M 11 |
| NE | Northeast | U 5 | Racon | Radar responder beacon | M 12 |
| N'Ly | Northerly | Fq | Ra (conspic) | Radar conspicuous object | M 14 |
| NM | Notice to Mariners | F 42 | RA DOME | Radar dome | Mh |
| No | Number | E 23 | Ra Ref | Radar reflector | Lf; M 13 |
| Np | Neap tide | T 7 | RBHB | Red and black horizontal | |
| NW | Northwest | U 8 | | bands | L 17, 18, 19, 20, 20a |
| NWS | National Weather Service | | R Bn | Red beacon | L 52 |
| | Signal Station | Jb | R Bn | Radiobeacon | M 3, 4, 16 |
| **O** | | | Rd | Radiolaria | S 35 |
| OBSC | Obscured (light) | K 68 | rd | Red | S 63 |
| Obs Spot | Observation spot | D 4 | Rd | Road, Roadstead | B 14; H 1 |
| Obstr | Obstruction | O 27 | RD | Directional Radiobeacon, | |
| Obsy | Observatory | J 21 | | Radio range | M 5 |
| Occ | Occulting (light), | | RDF | Radio direction finding station | M 7 |
| | Occultation | K 22, 46 | REF | Reflector | K 10; L 64 |
| Occ | Intermittent (light) | K 48 | Rep | Reported | O 35 |
| Occas | Occasional (light) | F 39; K 70 | Restr | Restricted | Fv |
| Off | Office | J 22 | Rf | Reef | O 23 |
| Or, or | Orange | K 65; L48b; S 62 | Rge | Range | B 27 |
| OVHD | | | RGE | Range | Kg |
| PWR CAB | Overhead power cable | H 4 | Rk | Rock | B 35 |
| Oys | Oysters, Oyster bed | S 24; G 15a | Rk, rky | Rock, Rocky | S 11 |
| Oz | Ooze | S 4 | Rky | Rocky | Bh |
| **P** | | | R MAST | Radio mast | M 9 |
| P | Pebbles | S 9 | Rot | Rotating (light), Revolving | K 31 |
| P | Pillar (buoy) | L 8a | RR | Railroad | H 3 |
| P | Pond | Bb | R RELAY MAST | Radio relay mast | Mb |
| P | Port | B 17; G 5 | R Sta | Radio telegraph station, | |
| PA | Position approximate | O 41 | | QTG Radio station | M1, 10a |
| | | | RT | Radio telephone station | M 2 |

# Abbreviations

| | | | | | |
|---|---|---|---|---|---|
| rt | Rotten | S 48 | T | Telephone | I 70; L 22c |
| R TR | Radio tower | M 9 | T | True | U 22 |
| Ru | Ruins | I 40 | T | Tufa | S 19 |
| RW<br>Bn | Red and white beacon | L 52 | TB | Temporary buoy | L 30 |
| | | | Tel | Telegraph | I 27; L 22b |
| Rv | Railway | H 3 | Telem Ant | Telemetry antenna | Ma |
| **S** | | | Tel Off | Telegraph office | I 28 |
| S | Sand | S 2 | Temp | Temporary (light) | F 38; K 73 |
| S | South; Southern | U 3, 11 | ten | Tenacious | S 55 |
| S | Spar (buoy) | L 8 | Thoro | Thorofare | B 9 |
| Sc | Scoriae | S 20 | Tk | Tank | I 53 |
| Sch | Schist | S 13a | TR | Tower | I 41 |
| Sch | School | I 65 | TRLB, TRUB, | TLB, TUB | Ki, j, k, l |
| Sd | Sound | B 8 | Tri | Triangulation | D 10 |
| SD | Sounding doubtful | Q 1 | TV TR | Television tower (mast) | M 9a |
| SE | Southeast | U 6 | | | |
| sec, s | Second (time; geo. pos.) | E 3; Kd | **U** | | |
| SEC | Sector | K 49 | uhf | Ultra high frequency | Mi |
| Sem | Semaphore | J 10 | Uncov | Uncovers; Dries | O 2, 32, 34 |
| S Fl | Short flashing (light) | K 25a | Univ | University | Ih |
| sft | Soft | S 41 | unverd | Unverified | Fb |
| Sh | Shells | S 23 | unev | Uneven | S 71 |
| Shl | Shoal | O 22 | μsec, μs | Microsecond (one millionth) | Eb |
| Sig Sta | Signal station | J 9 | | | |
| SIREN | Fog siren | N 11 | **V** | | |
| Sk | Stroke | Fu | var | Variation | U 24 |
| S-L Fl | Short-long flashing (light) | K 28a | vard | Varied | S 70 |
| Slu | Slough | Be; C 18 | VB | Vertical beam | Kf |
| S'ly | Southerly | Fr | vel | Velocity | T 23 |
| sml | Small | F4; S 44 | Vert | Vertical (lights) | K 80 |
| Sn | Shingle | S 8 | VERT CL | Vertical clearance | H 18a |
| Sp | Spring tide | T 6 | vhf | Very high frequency | Mi |
| SP | Spherical (bouy) | L 7 | Vi, vi | Violet | K 61; S 68 |
| Spg | Sponge | S 26 | View X | View point | D 6 |
| Spi | Spicules | S 31 | Vil | Village | I 3 |
| S'PIPE | Standpipe | I 45 | Vol | Volcanic | S 16 |
| spk | Speckled | S 50 | Vol Ash | Volcanic ash | Sb |
| S Sig Sta | Storm signal station | J 11 | VS | Vertical stripes | L 32 |
| St | Saint | F 11 | | | |
| St | Street | I 26 | **W** | | |
| St | Stones | S 10 | W | West, Western | U 4, 12 |
| Sta | Station | J 1, 2 | W, wh | White | K 67; L 41; S 56 |
| std | Standard | F 32 | W<br>Bn | White beacon | L 52 |
| stf | Stiff | S 43 | | | |
| Stg | Sea-tangle | S 29 | Wd | Seaweed | S 28 |
| stk | Sticky | S 46 | Whf | Wharf | G 18 |
| St M, St Mi | Statute mile | Ea | WHIS | Fog whistle | N 15 |
| Str | Strait | B 7 | Wk | Wreck | O 15, 28 |
| Str | Stream | Bc; T 17 | Wks | Wrecks, Wreckage | O 29 |
| str | Streaky | S 49 | W Or | White and orange | Le |
| sub | Submarine | F 20 | W'ly | Westerly | Ft |
| SUB-BELL | Submarine fog bell | N 5, 6 | | | |
| Subm, subm | Submerged | F 33; Oa, 30 | **Y** | | |
| Subm Ruins | Submerged ruins | Gd | Y, yl | Yellow | L 24, 44; S 61 |
| SUB-OSC | Submarine oscillator | N 7 | yd | Yard | E 8 |
| Sub Vol | Submarine volcano | O 8 | | | |
| Subm W | Submerged Well | Ob | 1st | First | Fj |
| SW | Southwest | U 7 | 2nd, 2d | Second | Fk |
| sw | Swamp | B 1 | 3rd, 3d | Third | Fl |
| | | | 4th | Fourth | Fm |
| **T** | | | ° | Degree | E 20 |
| t | Tonne | E12a | ' | Minute (of arc) | E 21 |
| T | Ton | E i | " | Second (of arc) | E 22 |

# AIDS TO NAVIGATION ON NAVIGABLE WATERS
## except Western Rivers and Intracoastal Waterway

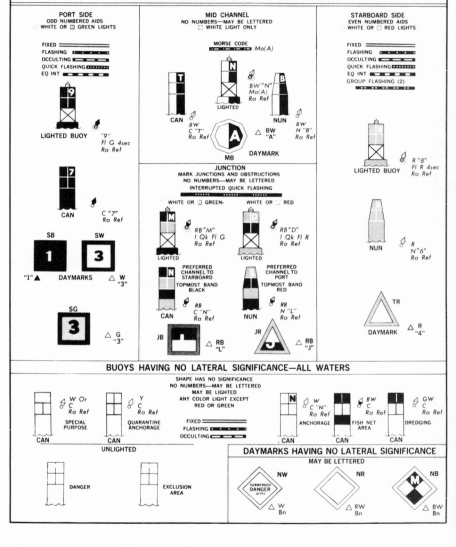

# AIDS TO NAVIGATION ON THE INTRACOASTAL WATERWAY

## AS SEEN ENTERING FROM NORTH AND EAST—PROCEEDING TO SOUTH AND WEST

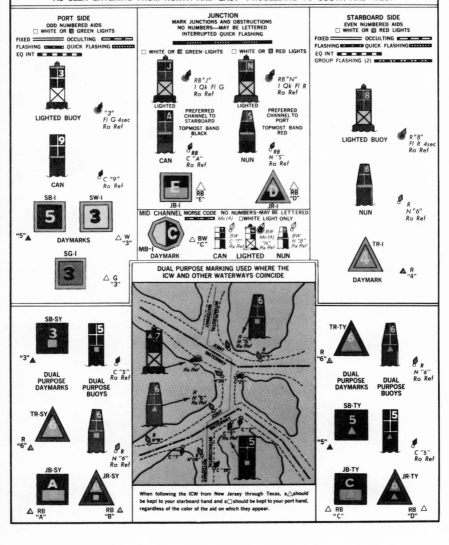